# God is Not
# Black-and-White

# God is Not
# Black-and-White

### Seeking Unity in a
### Theologically Diverse Church

## Robert Snitko

WIPF & STOCK · Eugene, Oregon

Wipf & Stock
An Imprint of Wipf and Stock Publishers
199 W. 8th Ave., Suite 3
Eugene, OR 97401

www.wipfandstock.com

PAPERBACK ISBN: 978-1-5326-3907-4
HARDCOVER ISBN: 978-1-5326-3908-1
EBOOK ISBN: 978-1-5326-3909-8

Manufactured in the U.S.A.                                    12/22/17

This book is dedicated to my incredible wife,
Mags.
You have constantly supported,
encouraged, and challenged me
throughout the process of writing this book.
Thank you for your unfailing love towards me.

The central Christian belief is that Christ's death has somehow put us right with God and given us a fresh start. Theories as to how it did this are another matter. A good many different theories have been held as to how it works; what all Christians are agreed on is that it does work.

—C.S. Lewis in *Mere Christianity*

# Contents

# Preface

I WANT TO ADDRESS the nonbeliever that is reading this book, who perhaps has left because of the mess that exists within the church. Perhaps you have been wronged by the church and you are experiencing hurt and pain. I want you to know, that this book is for you. The church has been—more than I want to admit—hurtful, unaccepting, judgmental, and hypocritical, among other things, towards many. This could be you. And I want you to know, this book is for you. Because within the church itself, there are many issues that transpire on a day-to-day basis. Even when considering all aspects of God and about God. But for you, non-Christian, I want you to know that the hope is to bring restoration within the church as we unite in the gospel of Jesus Christ, which has power to heal our brokenness, the power to heal our wickedness, the power to restore our relationships, the power to teach us how to truly love again, and the power to ask for forgiveness, as it is freely given to us in Christ Jesus.

I want to acknowledge the nonbeliever that has never believed. Maybe it's because you cannot fathom the existence of God, so you choose not to believe. Maybe you cannot wrap your mind around the wickedness in this world, and how a loving God can allow all of these things to transpire. Maybe, for you, just as the nonbeliever who has been hurt by the church—you too have been hurt by the hypocrisy and division that is caused between the church and those outside of the church. I want to welcome you into a restoring narrative of how Christians themselves have wronged each other as well. The truth is that there is way too much disunity going on in the world—and the church should not be participating in these habits as well. Whatever your struggles, what ever your battles, whatever your doubts, know this: there is a church just for you that will embrace you into their arms and walk alongside of you. I encourage you to step out of your comfort zone and just ask God to show you where that church may be. This might just be the first leap of faith, or a step out of your comfort zone, that you take in this journey called life. Part of life is taking risks, and I would like to ask you to at least consider giving the church an opportunity. And know this—the church loves you, the church cares for you, the church is longing to share exactly why Jesus came, and that is to show love towards one another. And on behalf of the church, I want to say sorry. Sorry for making you believe that there is hate between the church and those outside of the church. May this book show you that there is much brokenness that exists within the church itself and that this brokenness is also in need of healing and restoration.

To the Christian—my hope is that this book challenges, encourages, and provokes a heart of openness in your thinking about the many things regarding theology. Let us consider those who are in deep need of healing and salvation before we look to seek division in our theological conceptualizations. It is simple for a church to divide based on theological disagreements, but it is far more glorifying to God when we pursue unity within our diversity.

Finally, let us welcome *all* into our places of worship, allowing *all* to experience the very grace that has been offered to us in Christ.

# Acknowledgments

FIRST AND FOREMOST I would like to acknowledge my beautiful wife, Mags, for always challenging, encouraging, and supporting me in my writing. You truly are the most incredible woman as you resemble the very image of God in your character. Thank you for always pushing me to work harder while shedding the light of Christ in our family. You truly are a blessing from the Lord, and I am grateful for every moment with you.

I would like to acknowledge Zach Wright. In this journey of dialoguing about theological diversity you have continued to challenge me in my thinking. I really believe our bitter church experiences have shaped who we are today in Christ. Thank you for always sharing your brilliant thinking with me. If it weren't for you I don't know if I would have even attempted to write this book. Let's continue this journey of dialoguing about the depths and mysteries of God.

I am grateful as well for my college roommate and forever friend, David Prussia. The conversations during our undergraduate studies have encouraged me that no matter what, the gospel of Christ is what holds everything together. I also want to thank you for having the difficult conversations with me as we struggled together in one of the most formative times of our lives.

# Introduction

DURING MY UNDERGRADUATE STUDIES at Moody Bible Institute, I began to love theology since it allowed me to comprehend the depth and beauty of God. Or did it? Can I truly comprehend the depths of God and who he is? I thought so. I became so passionate about theology that my friends and I would stay up into the wee hours of the night in our dorm room talking about all things God: his character, attributes, majesty, love, and all of who he is. In my four years of Bible college, do you think I figured God out? As mentioned above, I thought I did. By my junior year, I had compartmentalized God and certain things about him that I believed, knowing no one would win an argument against me and my theology. This became more and more real in my heart, to the point that I would occasionally get into arguments, perhaps even fights (not fist fights) with some of my classmates about God. The more I did this, the more I was convinced that my ideologies of God were the only ideologies that were correct about him. Others were simply wrong and that's just the way it was. I was glad to know the "real" God, because my classmates had no clue about him. And so this is what I thought the study of God was; once you think you've figured him out, you've figured him out. To me, God was simply black-and-white in who he is (his attributes), his instruction for the church today (doctrine), and what I believe about him (my theology). The more I thought like this, the more critical I was of everyone's theology.

After graduating from Moody, I started seminary where I was in the midst of others whose theology differed from mine. Immediately, I began to tense up and get my boxing gloves out. There was no way these people were right about God and what he says in the Scriptures. I had a difficult time in class as I was trying to keep my cool in the midst of other people's perspectives on God. On my way home that first night of seminary, I was deeply convicted. God had revealed my pride to me unlike ever before. I couldn't understand why at that moment, but God called me out. I realized that my dogmatic approach to *secondary issues* in theology had actually distanced me from the people of God. Just to be clear, secondary issues are theologies in Scripture that are not completely clear, leading to many differing perspectives.

As the body of Christ, we ought to dwell together in unity for the sake of the gospel (Ps 133:1). Instead of constantly fighting with others regarding *secondary issues*, I was convicted to ask questions like "why do you believe what you believe?" and "how did you come to that conclusion?" Before, I was searching to find victory in a theological debate due to my pride and arrogance; since then however, things have drastically shifted. The more I took this to God, the more he began to soften my heart to theological diversity, a willingness to embrace someone else's perspective on God for the sake of love, the knowledge that others come to theological conclusions that are different than mine, and that is okay. I began to think about my childhood, where I saw way too many churches divide because of secondary issues. And not only the division of churches, but the severing of relationships. How is this in any way, shape, or form how God is calling us to live as Christians? These are questions that constantly came up in this heart-softening process. As I continued to pray for a softened heart it started to become clear to me that maybe God can't be figured out as much as I want to figure him out. Maybe the Spirit of God speaks to each person in his own way for their personal and communal edification in Christ, for the glory of God. Maybe, just maybe, God is not black-and-white even though many assume he is. Maybe God is a God of mystery and wants to remain that way so we might constantly yearn to seek him and his beauty. As the body of Christ, the church, we ought to seek unity in diversity so we may learn to love one another the way Christ loves us.

In this book, I look to address that God indeed is not black-and-white when dealing with secondary issues, or doctrines. There are many gray areas regarding theology. What I may think about God may be completely different than what you think about God. And guess what? It is completely okay to disagree. But how can we disagree in love? How can our theological conversations unite us, rather than divide us, especially when it comes to secondary issues? This is my heart behind writing this book; I am longing for unity within the local church and the church at large. Many churches split because of secondary issues and these splits cause division, hurt, and relational turmoil. How is this godly living? How can we restore our churches so they can love one another the way Christ called us to love one another? I think it begins with embracing one another's differences and theologies regarding secondary issues, because God is not black-and-white and his mystery is beautiful. Contrary to popular belief, I would argue that God is actually not black-and-white when it comes to many theological doctrines. The reasoning for this conclusion is the result of the many perspectives that exist in theological doctrines. What is clear is what God makes clear, which is that every being comprehends what God intends for him or her to understand. The rest is important, yet it is not as black-and-white as other doctrines or perspectives. The church must seek unity in diversity within the context of theology, so that love is at the epicenter of our theology.

I wrote *God is Not Black-and-White* because I've been around many people in the church who have a theological framework that is extremely diverse. I used to think these people were all wrong—I mean, how could someone not be a reformed Calvinist (this is who I was)? Unless people held to a reformed Calvinist perspective, to my mind they had theology all wrong. This book is intended to encourage the believer that not everyone comes from the same culture or context, and thus our theologies may and most often will be different from one another, and this is okay. So I humbly ask you to please join me in this journey of finding *shalom* (or "peace"), within the church, as we venture through the following chapters together.

# Chapter 1

# Why Theology?

For everything that was written in the past was written to teach
us, so that through the endurance taught in the Scriptures and
the encouragement they provide we might have hope.

—ROMANS 15:4

BEFORE WE DIALOGUE ABOUT the importance of theological diversity and agreeing to disagree on secondary issues, we must first
grasp the nature of theology itself. Why is theology necessary and
why is it important to us? I have had many conversations with
people who have said, "Why do we need theology when all we really need is Jesus?" I don't disagree with them regarding needing
Jesus, but I do believe that every believer needs theology and needs
to study theology. Merriam-Webster defines theology as the study
of religious faith, practice, and experience; *especially*: the study of
God and of God's relation to the world.[1] Thus theology is necessary
for all Christians as it is the study of our faith, practice, and experience of God. We study theology to know God more. We study
theology so that we may grow deeper in our love and relationship
with God. We study theology because we want to transform our
thinking by the renewing of our minds in order to understand the

1. https://www.merriam-webster.com/dictionary/theology.

will of God (Rom 12:2). We study theology so that we may be able to know how to defend our faith (apologetics) when confronted by those who do not believe, because the more we know about God and who he says he is, the more we will be able to defend our faith. Studying theology is essential to our understanding of God and who he is.

My wife, Maggie, and I got married while I was finishing up my undergraduate work. During this time, she was working as a nurse, while I was writing paper after paper, reading book after book. She would come home from work ready to dialogue with me about life, but I was ready to dialogue about theology. These two would not always go well with each other because I would overwhelm her with ideas, but in time our conversations led to a discovery that theology and life really do intertwine. She would frequently ask questions about the books I was reading. During these reading endeavors, I encouraged her to read a book I read for a theology class. She was hesitant at first because she thought reading theology was something I did because I had to for class (it's true). But she decided to dive into a book called *Delighting in the Trinity: An Introduction to the Christian Faith* by Michael Reeves. As she read this book, she would often share about how God was moving in her through this book. She read the pages slowly, as she didn't want to miss a single word and its impact on her life. After she finished the book, she told me that reading the book drew her closer to God, while deepening her relationship with him. I was overjoyed to hear the impact studying theology had on her personal walk with Christ. It changed her. It changed the way she thought about God. A.W. Tozer, a famous theologian, once said, "What comes into our minds when we think about God is the most important thing about us."[2] And how can we know what to think about God if we are not actively "doing" theology, or actively studying theology? Maggie experienced the depths of our triune God in a profound way. This resource led her to delve into the Scriptures as it affirmed her understanding of the most important

2. Tozer, *The Knowledge of the Holy*, 1.

things about God. The way she thought about God changed. And not only that—she changed.

Maggie experienced the importance of studying theology firsthand because through studying, her relationship with God grew. At first she did not recognize it, but after she completed the book she learned more about who God is, allowing her to draw near to him. It became evident to me that the reason we do theology is so we may draw near to God, as we experience his love for us, through our knowledge of him.

## Theology as Devotion

Theology is meant to be a devotional practice. It is meant to unite us to our Lord and Savior, Jesus Christ. The more we know about God, the more we can experience his person, his nature, and his love for us. This allows us to draw near to Him as we are united with Christ Jesus to fulfill the purpose of God. This is because God is profound and infinite. As we encounter him, we delve into the depths of who he is. Of course we can never fully figure God out (more in chapter four, *Mystery is Beautiful*), but God is able to equip us with profound knowledge of himself in our study of him. And as we study about him, we are able to enter into a place of worship, awe, wonder, and praise, and all while experiencing his presence through devotion, prayer, meditation, and worship. To study theology is to encounter God devotionally.

## Theology as a Way of Thinking

The study of theology is also very important when it comes to our thinking. Our thinking in general needs to be highly influenced by what we know about God, and what God says about everything we believe. Often times, our thinking is shaped by the world we live in. This is not necessarily a bad thing, but if we don't take the world's approach to all things life and refine it through the lens of God, then we have it all wrong. Whether it is ethical issues, moral issues, world views, or how to approach certain life decisions, the world can lead us in many false directions. But if we approach these things theologically, God will be honored through our lives. He will be glorified because our decisions will be based on what he has provided for us through his Scriptures. We study theology so it can shape the way we think about all things life and the decisions we make.

## Theology as Faith Defense

Studying theology is also critical to our understanding of the very faith we have. God has given us this faith, and he has graced us with his Son, Jesus Christ, so we may enjoy the riches of eternal life in him. For those who believe this, believe that this is good news. The good news is the gospel, and Jesus commanded that all those who have faith in him ought to share this very truth so the gospel may be made known throughout the world. This is Jesus' plea in the Gospel of Matthew when he states:

> All authority in heaven and on earth has been given to me. Therefore go and make disciples of all nations, baptizing them in the name of the Father and of the Son and of the Holy Spirit, and teaching them to obey everything I have commanded you. And surely I am with you always, to the very end of the age. (Matt 28:18-20)

It is important that believers are sharing this very gospel of Jesus Christ, as it has been revealed to them by the power of the Holy Spirit.

We have this power which gives us faith as a way of trusting in Christ, but the majority of the world does not like to believe in God by faith alone. Because of this, the world gets defensive and strategically attempts to structure arguments that will challenge the Christian. In doing so, many Christians have a difficult time explaining why they believe what they believe to non-Christians. Though faith is pleasing to the eyes of God, believers ought to be able to defend their faith in Christ to the nonbeliever. What is important to know is that this must be done in love and not out of anger. But the question is, how can a believer know how to defend their faith? How can a believer know what God says about himself? Studying theology will allow the believer to know more about the God they serve and worship. Therefore studying theology is critical to one's understanding of who God is and how he has decided to reveal himself. And the more God reveals himself to us, the more we are equipped to defend truth in the midst of a world that opposes it.

## Theology as Understanding Humanity

Theology is crucial to understanding humanity. One cannot know the true meaning of humanity apart from understanding it in the context of God's intent behind creating humanity. This means in order to understand who we are as human beings, we must first understand who our Creator is. We see in the Genesis account that God created man and woman in his image (Genesis 1:27), thus humanity bears the image of God. Of course, this image has been marred by the partaking of sin (Genesis 3), yet God, in his love, has provided a way to redeem the brokenness of sin. God incarnated himself into our very own depraved humanity so our image might be redefined in the Son of God, Jesus Christ. Our humanity is best understood in the incarnation of Christ (more on this later). If we don't study theology, then we will not fully comprehend the depths of our humanity. The study of theology in regard to understanding humanity is very important as we grasp the reality of being the very image-bearers of God in Christ Jesus.

## Final Thoughts

We study theology so we may learn more about God and who he is, which will ultimately lead us into a deeper relationship with him through Christ by the Holy Spirit. There are theologies that are black-and-white in the Scriptures. I like to refer to these theologies as primary theologies, or primary issues. These are theologies we all have to get right and which God reveals to his people. These theologies are straightforward and convincing to any and every Christian. But there are certain theologies in the Scriptures that are not so clear, things we want to know about God—yet do not—or wish the Bible was clearer on, because God is not black-and-white. I refer to these as secondary issues. Secondary issues are varying theological perspectives within the church that are important biblically, but are not a reason for our separation and division. Primary issues could very well be put in the category of the central doctrines within the church—whereas second-order doctrines could be referred to as "the rest." We begin to have a problematic experience in the church when secondary issues are viewed as dogma, or are expressed in a way where opinions somehow become "facts." Join me in the following chapter as we explore valid church dogmatics (primary doctrines), as opposed to second-order issues (secondary doctrines).

# Chapter 2

# Dogmatics vs. The Rest
# (Secondary Doctrines)

They claim to know God, but by their actions they deny him.
They are detestable, disobedient and unfit for doing anything
good. You, however, must teach what is appropriate to sound
doctrine.

—TITUS 1:16–2:1

WE LIVE IN A world that wants to have it all together. Within that reality, we develop a posture of dogma—where our authority over issues and ideas becomes the ultimate trump card. Dogma is what drives many people apart as they fall into the trap that its "my way or the highway." When it comes to one's understanding of theology, dogma can harm the development of doctrine simply because it can pertain to the close-mindedness of a theologian in an attempt to deny another's theological convictions. An openness in diverse thought must exist in order to allow the shaping of one's theological thought process.

It is important to understand what I mean by "dogmatics" and "the rest" here in the chapter title. For one, to be dogmatic means one's understanding about something cannot be altered or disputed. In other words, if you believe something about a certain topic or perspective, that belief is irrevocable (for the most part). I believe it is faithful to be dogmatic about primary doctrines in the church, but when dealing with secondary issues, or "the rest," we ought to be okay with agreeing to disagree in the church. So what are the primary doctrines that cannot be disagreed upon? And what are the secondary doctrines, or theological issues, that we can agree to disagree on?

## Front Porch

I had a great opportunity to meet with a pastor and friend, Mark, who discussed this idea of dogma in the church. During our conversation, he began explaining this idea of a front porch as being a place of dialogue, contemplation, and tension in our theological considerations. The idea is this: every front porch is very different and unique. Some porches have flowers, others have plants. Some have chairs, others have benches. Some are made up of different material, depending on preference. Front porches are unique in their aestheticism. Most front porches are also linked to a house, or some form of shelter—let's call this the *cornerstone*. The front porch is a space for dialogue, a dialogue where two or more can gather and share various thoughts and ideas with one another. These conversations do not change the fact the cornerstone exists in their midst. When the front porch talks conclude, and thoughts are stimulated, everyone returns back to the cornerstone. Within this cornerstone all have the main thing in common, that is, we are rooted in the same thing, the most important of them all. No matter the conversations, dialogues, or tensions that were encountered on the front porch, we all gather among the unity of the cornerstone. The point is this: there is space for a vast array of theological thought and conversation. These conversations could lead to profound discoveries about God and his goodness, but they also show that not everyone's theology is the same, which is not a bad thing. This is why many in the history of the church have so often disagreed when it comes to theology, thus demonstrating that God is not black-and-white when it comes to all things theology. These theological exchanges have led to iron-sharpening (Prov 27:17), as well as the refinement of one's thinking about God himself, but our thinking about God does not change who God is. Our thinking about God enables us to discern who we are in the eyes of God by way of the Holy Spirit. And this is why we have these various dialogues about God on our front porch. And at the end of the day we must always revert back to our cornerstone, who is Christ Jesus himself.

Regardless of our theological background or way of thinking, God will always be God. As we look at the root of our Christian faith, we must grasp the fact that what is essential to our church may not be essential to others. And so we must begin with a posture of rooting and grounding our Christian faith in the foundations of Christian faith, which first and foremost is Christ. Once we have established this cornerstone and grounding we may enter into the dialogue of what makes up our faith. The history of Christianity bids us to evaluate the foundation of our faith in regards to that which is primary. As we begin, we will evaluate the primary foundations and doctrines of the church by way of the Apostles' Creed.

## Apostles' Creed and Primary Doctrine

As we evaluate what primary doctrine consists of in regard to overall church doctrine, I think that it is important to allow the Apostles' Creed to serve as a basis for this foundation. For those unfamiliar with the Apostles' Creed, here is its declaration:

> I believe in God, the Father almighty, creator of heaven and earth. I believe in Jesus Christ, his only Son, our Lord, who was conceived by the Holy Spirit and born of the virgin Mary. He suffered under Pontius Pilate, was crucified, died, and was buried; he descended to hell. The third day he rose again from the dead. He ascended to heaven and is seated at the right hand of God the Father almighty. From there he will come to judge the living and

the dead. I believe in the Holy Spirit, the holy catholic[1] church, the communion of saints, the forgiveness of sins, the resurrection of the body, and the life everlasting. Amen.[2]

Within the very root of the Apostles' Creed we see the gospel of Jesus Christ as the creed affirms his sonship, lordship, as well as his suffering, crucifixion, death, resurrection, and ascension. The creed articulates the importance of the gospel narrative, as well as the life of Jesus. Next, we see the affirmation of the doctrine of the Trinity, as the Apostles' Creed emphasizes God as creator of heaven and earth, Jesus as Son, Lord, and Savior, and the Holy Spirit, as life-giver to all who believe. Finally, the Apostles' Creed affirms the incarnation of the Son of God, Jesus Christ. Through the conception of the Holy Spirit, God in Jesus Christ entered into the very humanity that we assume. This gave birth to the incarnation of God as the very flesh and blood of humanity was reflected in the incarnate Son of God. Jesus Christ was not only bearing the incarnate nature of humanity, but he was also fully divine, sharing in the full authority with God the Father.

As we access the difference between primary and secondary doctrines, let us remember to not place God in a doctrinal box, which can cause our dogmatic theology to be cemented in our hearts. Rather, let us maintain an open heart and open mind to the teachings of the Holy Spirit. I truly believe if we are sensitive to the Holy Spirit God will do a miraculous work in our lives. This miraculous work could perhaps develop a heart that is moldable to the work of God, rather than steeped in our own dogma, which can ultimately lead to division within the body of believers. Let us begin with the primary doctrines which stem from their association with the Apostles' Creed.

---

1. "Catholic" meaning the true Christian church of all times and all places.

2. "Apostles' Creed," https://www.crcna.org/welcome/beliefs/creeds/apostles-creed.

## Primary Doctrine: The Gospel

For one, we must start with the gospel of Jesus Christ. This doctrine affirms that Jesus Christ, the Son of God, incarnated humanity for the reconciliation and restoration of humanity's relationship with God Almighty (2 Cor 5:18). This doctrine affirms that in Christ's birth, life, ministry, death, resurrection, and ascension, broken sinners are renewed and restored into an eternal union with the Father, through the Son, by the Spirit (1 Pet 5:10). In this union, Jesus Christ shares his very being with his people, the church, in a bond unlike any other (John 14:20). Christ joins himself to the believer so the believer may have access to the Father (Eph 2:18). This is the beautiful harmony that is found in the gospel of Jesus Christ. This doctrine is one that we absolutely cannot disagree upon, because it is the very substance of the Christian faith. Thus to not affirm the gospel of Jesus Christ, is to not affirm Christianity.

The gospel is the essential need of every human being. All of humankind is born into a world of depravity and sin (Ps 51:1), and a direct separation from God is the result of this brokenness. God in his sovereign and faithful love for his precious creation sends his Son Jesus Christ so the sins of the world may be forgiven by his flesh and blood. God does this because he *loves* the creatures he created, and even though God's image-bearers have denied him time and time again he is faithful to forgive through the restoring grace of Christ Jesus, who is more powerful than the wickedness of God's image-bearers. Christ has reconciled human depravity in himself through the free gift of salvation, which is himself (Rom 5:15–17, ESV).

The very narrative of the gospel—which includes the conception, birth, life, death, burial, resurrection, and ascension of Jesus Christ—is what our hope is rooted in. Christ's life demonstrated the very life we ought to live, but because we assume a fallen nature through our birth into sin, we can hope in this Christ who came to set us free from slavery by offering us his very life for the forgiveness of sins. This free gift of the gospel is the mysterious grace of God. In Paul's letter to Ephesus, he writes,

For it is by grace you have been saved, through faith—
and this is not from yourselves, it is the gift of God—not
by works, so that no one can boast. For we are God's
handiwork, created in Christ Jesus to do good works,
which God prepared in advance for us to do. (Eph 2:8–10)

What a gift from the Creator of the universe! There is nothing
we have done to earn salvation. Salvation has been freely given to
us by the grace of God in His Son, Jesus Christ.

## Primary Doctrine: The Trinity

The doctrine of the Trinity is vital for, and must be affirmed by, the
church. The Trinity affirms that God is one in essence and three
in persons. This doctrine is derived from passages which affirm
that God is Creator (Gen 1:1); God in Christ is Savior (John 1:1–2;
14); and the Holy Spirit is God (Acts 5:3–4). The very substance
of God is found in the Trinity. It is important to understand the
Trinity and how God reveals himself in this way as this shapes our
primary doctrine, which is the Trinity. The process of God reveal-
ing himself is called progressive revelation. R.C. Sproul writes:

How, then, can we maintain the Old Testament doctrine
of monotheism in light of the clear New Testament affirmation of the triune character of the biblical God? Au-
gustine once wrote, "The New [Testament] is in the Old
[Testament] concealed; the Old is in the New revealed."
To understand how the doctrine of the Trinity came to
be such an important article of the Christian faith, we
need to see that there was a development of the church's
understanding of the nature of God based on the Scriptures. When we look into the Scriptures, we see what
we call in theology "progressive revelation." This is the
idea that, as time goes by, God unfolds more and more
of His plan of redemption. He gives more and more of
His self-disclosure by means of revelation. The fact that
there is this progress in revelation does not mean that
what God reveals in the Old Testament He then con-
tradicts in the New Testament. Progressive revelation is

not a corrective, whereby the latest unveiling from God rectifies a previous mistaken revelation. Rather, new revelation builds on what was given in the past, expanding what God has made known.[3]

Thus as time passes, the revelation of God as Trinity is unveiled to the believer, building upon what God has already made known. God is Father, Son, and Spirit. He is one God, yet three persons. And as Sproul mentions, as time has progressed, people in New Testament times and throughout history, as well as those who continue to teach the Scriptures faithfully, have seen the progressive revelation of God throughout the tapestry of themes in the biblical text.

To deny the Trinity is to deny who God is. Thus we must faithfully hold to the trinitarian theology of God as a primary understanding of who God is in the church. The Trinity resembles the unity that is found between the three persons in the trinity: Father, Son, and Holy Spirit. They are all one and share a significant union, which ought to be resembled and displayed in the lives of those who believe in him. The Trinity exists for the purpose of displaying what true communal living ought to be like, rather than me-centered living (more on this in the chapter to follow).

## Primary Doctrine: The Incarnation

The incarnation of God is a primary doctrine which is the hope of the Christian faith. But what is the doctrine of incarnation and why is it necessary in the church? One writer puts it this way:

> The Decree of Ecumenism situates the Church in the mystery of the Trinitarian communion of God and of the "mission" of the Son to the world, to "draw all things" to God. The communion of the faithful, in faith, hope, and charity, with the Body of Christ is a *koinonia* with the risen humanity of the Lord Jesus. In Jesus, God communes with humankind in his own body. By virtue of the

3. Sproul, *What is Trinity?*, 10–11.

resurrection, Jesus joins the *koinonia* of the incarnation to the *koinonia* of glorification.[4]

What is being articulated here is the incarnation of God in Christ Jesus joins the fellowship of all believers in order to achieve fellowship or communion with God in glorification. The incarnation of God is the very reason we have been redeemed and restored, through the perfect humanness of Christ.

Confessing the incarnation of Christ for the Christian alludes to that of which everything Christ has done in his humanity. Christ's humanity is the instrument of our very salvation as Christ himself is our salvation. In the very moment Christ entered into our humanity, he began his redeeming work. The incarnation is an essential component in the life of Christianity by way of Jesus sharing in the very humanity of flesh and blood, so that by these the enemy would be defeated (Heb 2:14). This is done so those who are held in slavery by their fear of death may be set free in the life of Christ (Heb 2:15). The author of Hebrews wraps up the purpose of the incarnation with astute clarity:

> For this reason He had to be made like them, fully human in every way, in order that He might become a merciful and faithful high priest in service to God, and that He might make atonement for the sins of the people. Because He Himself suffered when He was tempted, He is able to help those who are being tempted. (Heb 2: 17–18)

Let us rest in this truth of the incarnation; that Jesus has come to bear the very image of God—which is perfect—because humanity fell short of God's intentions. In the incarnation of Christ, humanity is restored to God the Father. Apart from the incarnation, Christianity would not be the same. Our image would not have been restored. But God in his grace has sent his Son in order to restore the image of all mankind.

---

4. Gros, et al., *Introduction to Ecumenism*, 60.

## Second-Order Issues

Second-order issues are different in every context. These theological perspectives and approaches are very important, yet many view them differently. Regardless of the differing views and approaches people take toward these perspectives, the goal is to understand each other and the varying approaches so we may pursue unity within our theological diversities. Below, I will address just a few doctrines in the church that people heavily disagree on—which causes separation in the church. Of course there are a number of other secondary doctrines the church wrestles with, but these are some of the most popular ones, and in addressing these my hope is the general sense of theological differences is drawn out for better understanding. We begin with the theology of the Lord's Supper.

## Eucharist (Lord's Supper)

The Lord's Supper is another sacrament that is practiced in the church. This sacrament is often referred to as a way of remembering the broken body and shed blood of Christ on the cross for the sins of the world. Most every single church participates in the Lord's Supper; the disagreement is often found in what the substance of the elements are. Leonard J. Vander Zee said, "The Lord's Supper became the focus of strong theological differences through church history, and these differences still affect how we understand the sacrament today."[5] The point here being that throughout the history of the church, many conclusions have been made regarding the Lord's Supper. During the Reformation period of the church in the sixteenth century, there was a heavy disunity at the table. Many of the leaders during the Reformation split because of the variety of perspectives about the Lord's Supper and what takes place during the participation of this sacrament.[6]

Within the Roman Catholic Church context, the Lord's Supper is perceived as an essential sacrament for the sustainment of

5. Vander Zee, *Christ, Baptism, and the Lord's Supper*, 161.
6. Ibid., 162.

the Catholic Church. Through this sacrament, the Church inherits the body and blood of Christ in its physical form, as the physical presence of Christ is consumed. The term for this is *transubstantiation*. This is where the bread and wine are consecrated by the priest, which alters the elements from being bread and wine as they become the physical body and blood of Jesus Christ.[7] When church historian Martin Luther came across the idea of transubstantiation, he found the doctrine to be both biblically and philosophically unsupportable.[8] Luther didn't object that Christ was present within the elements at the table, instead, Luther was concerned with the "how," regarding the presence of Christ in the Lord's Supper. Stephen J. Nichols writes:

> Theologians and historians often describe Luther's view as *consubstantiation*. This means that Christ, in substance, is with (from the Latin prefix con) the elements. This view stands opposed to the Catholic view designated *transubstantiation*, where the elements change, from the Latin prefix *trans*, to the very body or blood of Christ.[9]

Luther's disagreement with the Roman Catholic Church resulted in his own view and interpretation of the Lord's Supper. This view encouraged that Christ is present in, with, and by the elements. When he was asked how this is the case, Luther always answered that it is a mystery and paradox.

Another Reformer in the sixteenth century was French theologian John Calvin. Calvin himself had a whole other interpretation of the presence of Christ in the elements. Unlike Roman Catholicism or Luther, who argued for some sort of physical presence, Calvin understood there was a spiritual presence of Jesus Christ that existed among the Lord's Supper. Calvin believed the Supper is, "instituted by God as a gift from the hand of Christ. It is a spiritual feast by which Christ testifies that He Himself is living bread (John 6:51), on which our souls feed, for a true and blessed

7. Nichols, "Transubstantiation and Eucharistic Presence," 57.
8. Vander Zee, *Christ, Baptism, and the Lord's Supper*, 173.
9. Nichols, *Martin Luther*, 119.

immortality."[10] Contrary to Roman Catholicism's and Luther's views, Calvin did not believe in a physical manifestation of the elements; rather, he believed Christ was present in the elements spiritually, bringing about nourishment and satisfaction to the church through the gospel (body and blood). In partaking of the Lord's Supper, the Christian would encounter a spiritual fulfillment of satisfaction in Christ Jesus.

Finally, the Baptist tradition held to a memorial approach of the Lord's Supper. It has been said by the Baptist tradition that in order to understand the symbolism of the Lord's Supper, we must first take into account the biblical pattern of signs, and how it relates to the various roles of proclamation for the creation and sustenance of faith.[11] The Baptist tradition associates many of their practices with a remembrance-and-memorial approach, which thus applies to the sacraments of communion and baptism. Russell D. Moore gives a better understanding on this perspective though, stating it is not simply a remembrance or memorial:

> The very term *memorial* can be misleading. Many contemporary Christians have thus chafed at the idea of the Supper as a bare means to remembrance—prompting even some Baptists to embrace a more sacramental understanding of the Supper. But the historic Baptist concept of the Lord's Supper serves less as a "memorial" than as a sign—a sign pointing both backward and forward.[12]

He continues by noting:

> The sign nature of the Supper is in continuity then with the rest of God's redemptive purposes in the canon, purposes that often are linked with the concept of eating and feeding.[13]

The point is that unlike the Reformed or Catholic traditions, the Baptist tradition views the Lord's Supper as more of a sign and

10. Calvin, *Institutes of the Christian Religion*, 896.
11. Engle, et al., *Understanding Four Views on the Lord's Supper*, 29.
12. Ibid., 30.
13. Ibid., 30.

symbol. This view has been both rooted in Baptist tradition and confession.

Church history's tension regarding the view of the Lord's Supper has influenced the church today, as the church continues to view the meaning of the sacrament in various ways. Those who have strong beliefs regarding the Lord's Supper will avoid going to a church which does not represent their conviction. Some may even base their selection of church solely on which traditional view of the Lord's Supper is held. History's disagreements regarding the sacrament have come a long way as many churches affirm a variety of traditions in regard to their participation in the Lord's Supper. The point is this: we can disagree on how the Lord's Supper is taken or perceived, yet we should do so in love. Let us listen to one another in the various approaches that are taken to arrive at a particular conclusion regarding the Lord's Supper. Let us be a church which enters into a conversation that is intended to unite, as opposed to quickly telling others their view is wrong because we think we are correct.

## Worship Style: Liturgical/Traditional, Contemporary, and Charismatic

It is important to address that worship is not a secondary issue, but it is the style of worship that is being discussed here. Many churches worship in different ways. In fact, many people select which church they will attend based on the style of worship that the church offers. Traditionally speaking, churches have chosen to have their worship services emphasize a liturgical style of worship. These worship services may include a vast array of music, but mostly their music will emphasize hymns. Liturgy focuses on a traditional order of worship which may be appealing to a lifelong churchgoer, although many young people are also interested in liturgy as it is faithful to church history.

Another common worship style is the contemporary approach. This approach is more focused on providing an ease for those who are unfamiliar with the church, as things are brought about in a more modern fashion. Worship services will include up-to-date contemporary Christian songs, ones that are heard on the local radio station. These churches usually appeal to those who have moved on from the more traditional view and have sought out something that is more to their liking. This is not always the case as some transition because it is more appealing to their personality. Contemporary churches tend to be more seeker-sensitive, as they relate more with the non-Christian.

A final worship style is charismatic worship. In this worship style, many theological perspectives which vary from the traditional sense are at the forefront of what causes this style of worship. People tend to be more expressive in their worship. Some speak in various tongues, others dance, some even spend time asking God for healing of sickness. One can experience a more vibrant and diverse approach to a worship service in attending a charismatic church. This is a very different approach to worship than someone affiliated with a traditional style, or even a contemporary style of worship.

Whether a church is focused more on a liturgical, contemporary, or charismatic style of worship service does not mean that any of them are wrong. While many will argue that one is better than the other, it's not. It is a matter of personal preference. The point is this should not be a reason we are divided in the church. We can choose which churches we would like to attend, yet when we have conversations regarding which service is right or wrong, we need to be mindful of each other's perspectives. We need to have a conversation that will bring edification to one another as Christians, rather than tear each other up because of how we worship. Just because someone disagrees does not mean the worship style is wrong. Various worship styles that happen to be different from ours are still profound in their own ways. Let us now have a conversation regarding unique worship styles, and let us admire the ways we worship our heavenly Father.

## Ordination of Women in Ministry

Oftentimes, when dealing with the roles men and women should play in the church, many disagree due to a variety of interpretations in Scripture. It seems to be very clear that God has appointed a leadership structure or government when it comes to the church.[14] Various roles of church government include the pastorate, apostleship, eldership, and diaconate, among others. As this framework is established by the church, the differing roles for men and women come into question. I believe men and women in the church are equal in the eyes of God, as they are created in his image. When it comes to leadership in the church, it is evident to me that God can use a man or a woman in any way needed to bring glory to himself while edifying the body of Christ. Therefore, I would argue that men and women may have different roles in the church, but both can be used in any capacity necessary to bring glory to God. In other words, if a women must preach the word of God before the congregation, so be it. If the Holy Spirit has empowered her to teach and she can faithfully uphold the word of God, then I don't see why God can't use her in that aspect. The same goes with men. If God has empowered a man to teach the word of God faithfully, then the man shall obediently deliver God's word to the congregation.

## Various Roles of Men and Women in the Bible: Apostle

There are many leadership roles in the church, especially those outlined in Ephesians 4 where Paul is addressing the unity in the body of Christ. These keys roles include apostles, prophets, evangelists, shepherds, and teachers (Eph 4:11). These roles were given by Christ for the equipping of saints in the work of ministry, in order to build up the body of Christ (Eph 4:12). There is no indication in this passage that these key roles were specifically and only given to men or women. It appears to be addressing the church at large. One problem that could stem from this is apostleship, specifically

14. Allison, *Sojourners and Strangers*, 205.

because we have the apostles that followed Jesus, meaning that women could not possibly be apostles. From the complementarian perspective, this argument seems to be valid as there does not seem to be any recordings of women apostles. Although, from an egalitarian approach, Paul, the writer of Romans, clearly acknowledge a woman who was outstanding among the apostles. Paul writes, "Greet Andronicus and Junia, my fellow Jews who have been in prison with me. They are outstanding among the apostles, and they were in Christ before I was" (Rom 16:7). Perhaps not a clear utterance of Junia being an apostle per se, but there is something special in the language Paul uses to acknowledge that Junia was indeed outstanding among the apostles.[15] In Jesus' time, there were apostles, and as we look at the church today, all who believe in the gospel seem to immediately become an apostle in one form or another, as an apostle is one who is sent out. As Jesus mentioned in the Great Commission, those who are in Christ are summoned to make disciples of all nations, baptizing in the name of the Father, Son, and Spirit (Matt 28:19).

## Prophet

The next role that is mentioned in Ephesians is prophets. Biblical accounts have recorded both men and women in the roles of prophets (messengers of God's word). We see in the Old Testament that a women named Miriam is referred to as a prophet (Exod 15:20). This indicates she was speaking the word of God to the people of God, meaning she was speaking to both men and women. Along with Miriam, Deborah, a judge from the book of Judges is referred to as a prophet as well (Judg 4:4). What stands out about Deborah is that under the old covenant, she had much power as a judge and a prophet. Just as women were prophets in the Old Testament, we see men as prophets all throughout the Scriptures. There was Jeremiah, Isaiah, Moses, Daniel, David, Ezekiel, Amos, Malachi, John the Baptist, etc. This helps us see that even in biblical times,

---

15. McKnight, *The Blue Parakeet*, 179–80.

roles were shared between men and women. God still uses men and women to articulate his truth, and he used to speak to our ancestors through the prophets, but today he speaks to us through his Son (Heb 1:1–2). The truth of his Son can be spoken of by both male and female.

## Evangelists, Shepherds, and Teachers

Biblically speaking, the first account of evangelism that is seen starts at the tomb of Jesus Christ himself. The women took spices to the tomb of Christ to put beside his body (Luke 24:1). Mary Magdalene and the other Mary went to the tomb (Matt 28:1) and noticed that the stone was rolled away and that Jesus Christ was not there (Matt 28:6). An angel appeared and told the women to go and tell the disciples about this situation, thus these women were the first ever evangelists (Matt 28:7). Jesus himself appeared to the women and told them to go and tell his brothers about his resurrection (Matt 28:10). Women were used by God to share the gospel message in the New Testament.[16] This is the same case with men. Men are constantly used throughout the New Testament to share the gospel of Christ. Peter addresses the crowd in Acts 2, sharing the good news of Jesus Christ so that many would come to believe. Likewise, Paul is a figure who is constantly sharing the good news of Jesus Christ. Once a persecutor of Christians and destroyer of the church (Acts 8:3), Paul himself was transformed by the gospel of Christ (Acts 9:1–31) and was an evangelist ever after.

Shepherds and teachers are also key functions of church leadership today. The New Testament gives us many examples of those who were shepherds and those who were teachers. Priscilla and Aquila were apostolic extenders of the gospel who were trained and sent by Paul to plant churches. Priscilla and Aquila's roles in the New Testament church seem to have been pretty similar to one another. Apollos was a man of education and status in the New Testament, thus it is clear that the influence of Priscilla and Aquila

16. Elwell and Beitzel, *Baker Encyclopedia of the Bible*, 1883.

on his life were vital in their ministry. Today, men and women teach in various roles within the church, and God uses both for the knowledge and edification of his word.

Women in ministry is a sensitive subject in the church (especially in fundamentalist circles), but it is important to address this issue. Many completely dismiss this issue, whereas others worry about bringing it up, knowing it could potentially mar a relationship. Now I am not trying to argue for which side one should choose; rather, I am highlighting an ongoing issue in the church: disunity. And when it comes to women in ministry, many disagree, argue, and split up, due to hardened and stubborn hearts. Is it okay to be complementarian? Yes. Is it okay to be egalitarian? Yes. Should we split because of our differing views? No. Mature believers must pursue the conversation of unity within our theological diversity. When it comes to our views of women and their roles in the church, many people have various approaches to this issue. Some are for women in ministry, others are against it. Regardless of one's approach to this issue, we must be settled on love, which will ultimately keep us united in the gospel, as we share in the body and blood of Jesus Christ. We must seek to be one as Christ originally intended. Paul wrote in his letter to Ephesus that:

> Christ himself gave the apostles, the prophets, the evangelists, the pastors and teachers, to equip his people for works of service, so that the body of Christ may be built up until we all reach unity in the faith and in the knowledge of the Son of God and become mature, attaining to the whole measure of the fullness of Christ. (Eph 4:11-13)

If the gospel is important to us, we must seek reconciliation in our relationships and not bicker about being right all the time. The gospel must change us for the glory of God and his kingdom to be made known in our very churches and communities.

## Final Thoughts on Dogmatics vs. The Rest

Sacraments are very important in the church as they were instituted by Christ himself. Much like the Lord's Supper, baptism is a vital sacrament which is crucial to the growth and sustenance of the church, but whose application in regards to frequency of use is the cause of much debate among Christians. We didn't spend much time talking about baptism, but the idea of this sacrament is similar to the Lord's Supper by way of disagreement. There are various views and many people disagree about how baptisms should be performed in the church. This sacrament has been practiced throughout the history of the church, and its disagreements rest in the way the church ought to baptize. Some churches baptize infants, which is symbolic to them, others prefer immersion (also symbolic), symbolizing the death to self and resurrection of one's spiritual journey.

We don't have the time to cover every second-order issue within the church, so I will briefly go through some other second-order issues churches disagree on. These include differing perspectives on the creation account ("Was it a literal seven-day creation or not?"). Did people in the Old Testament really live past five hundred years old? When dealing with the end times, when will Christ return? Will he have a literal, one-thousand-year reign on earth, or is it metaphorical? You get the idea. Many of these conclusions are assumed by our hermeneutics (interpretation of the Bible), which we also disagree on. Many Bible readers read the Bible differently. Some translate it to be literal, word-for-word; others read it narratively; some approach it allegorically, or metaphorically; some read it based on the various genres of the books; etc. The list goes on and on.

So the question is this: at the end of the day, who is right in their theological conclusions? What makes one person's theology better than another person's? How come there have been differing approaches in theology throughout the history of the church up until the times we live in today, if God is clear in what he says to people. I believe it is because God is not black-and-white regarding the second-order theological issues we are constantly disagreeing on, because if God was indeed black-and-white we would not have varying theological perspectives on second-order issues. Rather, we would all agree with one another, just as we do in Christian orthodoxy in regards to the gospel, the Trinity, and the incarnation of Christ.

I want to be clear when I say that second-order issues are very important to the church and its cultural significance, theological progression, spiritual development, and biblical importance. The push is for unity within the second-order issues in the church. The reason second-order issues exist is because they are not as clear as the primary doctrines. We disagree because there are many gray areas in the biblical text and there are insufficient solutions for every theological doctrine. What we can do best is seek to be as faithful as possible, understanding that we will not always get things right. If this were not true, then we would never disagree on second-order issues.

## Conclusion

When dogma is at the core of who we are in our secondary issues we can easily dismiss an individual who may see things differently than we do. Our differing perspectives do a good job of bringing about the exclusion of one another, as well as developing a heart that gets hardened against another's voice or theological framework. When used improperly, dogma can be a very hurtful approach towards doing theology in relation to second-order doctrines. These dogmas can be at the core of what tears the church apart, giving birth to brutal relational dysfunction within the body of Christ. C.S. Lewis said it best:

> The central Christian belief is that Christ's death has somehow put us right with God and given us a fresh start. Theories as to how it did this are another matter. A good many different theories have been held as to how

it works; what all Christians are agreed on is that it does work.[17]

Essentially what Lewis is articulating is that Christians understand the concept of what God has revealed. These concepts, however, are diverse in both thought and theory. These, Lewis says, are another matter. In the midst of the various theories and conclusions that come about, what Christians can all agree on is it worked. It happened. The ways we think about these theories possibly coming to fruition are endless, and it could even be that our theory on a theological assumption was wrong all along. Who knows? At best, we can only *assume* the results of theological conclusions based on our understanding of the Scriptures. This is why being diverse in our thinking can actually help our theological framework in a way that allows the Spirit to guide us in a direction of contemplation, to realize we could perhaps have it wrong. This will allow the Spirit of God to lead us into a posture of love for those who do not see things the way we do, ultimately bringing us into unity with other believers. This could then ultimately lead the bride of Christ back into the oneness it was intended for with the Bridegroom.

17. Lewis, *Mere Christianity*, 54.

# Chapter 3

# Divisive Love

And over all these virtues put on love, which binds them all
together in perfect unity.

—COLOSSIANS 3:14

A DOGMATIC PERSPECTIVE ON second-order issues of theology
could cause one to believe God cannot be outside that perspective, which may lead to a hardened heart to what the Spirit can do.
When we become dogmatic regarding second-order theological
perspectives, there is a high risk of creating disunity within the
church, a disunity that is unbiblical and focuses too much on the
perspective itself rather than the people who make up the body of
Christ. But what if the church responded to second-order theological issues in a way that would bring about the unity that is found
in Christ, rather than dividing in love?

Consider the following illustration: When my wife and I got
married, we moved into the heart of Chicago. During this season
we were looking for a church to call home. We did plenty of re-
search online and found many churches in the Chicagoland area.
We thought to ourselves, "where do we even begin?" We decided
to check out a particular church that was recommended to us by
a friend. At first, we didn't know what to think. But after a long

summer of consistent attendance, we felt like this was going to be our home church for that season of life. As we got more involved we decided to take a step towards membership. One of the neat aspects of this church's membership was we would have membership meetings semi-regularly. This allowed the church to dialogue about subjects like doctrine, vision, and any tensions that existed. This was a unique aspect of the church, as it allowed members to have open dialogue about things that would otherwise be ignored. During one of our first meetings, the pastor brought up the idea of what it would look like for women to serve in higher-capacity ministry roles. You could feel the tension in the room. From both parties involved. As the room was open for discussion, much time was spent in conversation and frustration. At the end of the meeting, it was confirmed there was an agreement to disagree, and it was okay to live in that tension as it brought about unity within the body of Christ in love, rather than a division without love.

## Divisive Love in the Gospel

The doctrine of the gospel seeks to bring about unity within the body of Christ. First, the gospel shows us the love of God. God cares about each and every person. His care is especially evident in the midst of our failure to obey him. In our disobedience, God was faithful to forgive humanity by sending his Son Jesus Christ in order to bring salvation into the world. Our sinful nature tends to be influenced by disunity, through a rebellious tendency of hatred toward one another. The real and life-giving gospel that is meant to bring unity among believers has been rejected by many as they have pursued their own versions and forms of the gospel. Some have clung to the poverty gospel. This gospel tells the believer that in order to fulfill the great commandment, one must sell all of their possessions and belongings, as this is how one faithfully stewards the gospel. This is an inaccurate representation of what the gospel truly is. The gospel isn't about selling all of your possessions and fleeing from any form of life other than poverty. The gospel is about experiencing the grace of God that is offered to us in Christ

Jesus, who offered up his life on the cross. And in his resurrection, he defeated the grave and gave us life everlasting in himself.

Another component of divisive love in the gospel is affirming the prosperity gospel. This gospel preaches that you will find wealth and riches if you give more money to the church that proclaims this false truth. I am not saying it is wrong to give to the church; in fact, it is completely biblical (2 Cor 9:7). But when prosperity becomes the focus of the church service, the gospel is being distorted, as if life in Christ is a life that will bring complete prosperity (materialistically) to the one who believes. Don't get me wrong, God will prosper the life of the believer in the physical and material sense if it is his will, but the sole pursuit of prosperity within our faith in Christ is a distortion of the gospel.

The gospel is love. And love is divided and distorted when the gospel is made anything other than love. The gospel is God's redemptive work in bringing reconciliation to his people in and through Jesus Christ. This is love. The gospel does not need to have an adjective that exists before it. The gospel is simply the gospel. The gospel is the restoration of love that has been betrayed by sinful humanity. Christ Jesus came to bring unity among the people of the world, so that we may best resemble the kingdom of God in our love toward one another.

## Divisive Love in the Trinity

God is the Trinity. We established this to be a primary doctrine in chapter 2. This is essential to who God is and his identity. To deny the Trinity is to deny the reality of who God really is. The Trinity is both who God is and a picture of who God calls us to be. God calls us to live in unity as believers, as this mirrors his very being and essence. Reformed theologian, R.C. Sproul, stated:

> Before we can talk about the Trinity, we have to talk about unity, because the word *Trinity* means "tri-unity." Behind the concept of unity is the biblical affirmation of monotheism. The prefix *mono* means "one or single," while the

root word *theism* has to do with God. So, *monotheism* conveys the idea that there is only one God.[1]

The main point Sproul is making is one that offers unity within the Trinity. The concept of unity is at the core of who the Trinity is. In other words, the very essence of God is one of unity. This unity is resembled in his tri-unity as Father, Son, and Holy Spirit. Apart from that unity, God is not who he says he is. Thus in order for us to understand God's intent for the unity of all people, we must first understand the unity he has with the Trinity.

The Trinity is the perfect example of how believers ought to live: in unity. In the Genesis narrative, God creates man and woman in his very image. What is interesting is the terminology that is used:

> Then God said, "Let us make mankind in our image, in our likeness, so that they may rule over the fish in the sea and the birds in the sky, over the livestock and all the wild animals, and over all the creatures that move along the ground." So God created mankind in his own image, in the image of God he created them; male and female he created them. (Gen 1:26–27)

God speaks in the Genesis narrative when he creates mankind. He says, "Let us make mankind in our image," and then does so (Gen 1:27). Here, the Hebrew word for God is *elohim*, which is a plural noun, followed by a singular verb of *creating*. Thus God is three, yet one. This very essence of who he is in the Trinity is the exact nature we were created to resemble. The key to the Trinity is unity, and the key to the life of believers is, likewise, unity. We must seek to find unity within the body of Christ as this is the very essence of who we were created to be: a united body of believers for the sake of the gospel. We mar the image of the Trinity through dismembering the body of believers. God created us to be unified in the gospel, as this resembles the very God who brought us into existence. God would not be God apart from the Trinity. And the body of Christ cannot be the body of Christ if we are constantly

1. Sproul, *What Is the Trinity?*, 2.

dismembering it with regard to our theological presuppositions on secondary issues.

Today's society is constantly pursing isolation. This has even shifted into church culture. People have stopped going to church because there is "nothing" to be offered by the church. Today's culture has shifted to being individualistic rather than communal, and the church is beginning to see the impact of this shift. An article on *Patheos* states that as of 2015, US church attendance had sunk to a record low, and the word used to refer to many who have left the church is "the Nones."[2] The Nones are those who do not categorize themselves as religious people and either do not attend church regularly or not at all. The danger behind this culture is the reality of dismembering the body of Christ. In today's culture, many are running away from the church and this is creating a divided body. The Nones are contributing to the dismembering of the church as they are seeking a greater social and cultural presence in the church, which they perceive to be lacking. Thus, the Nones are not finding their role in the body of Christ, which is contributing to their departure. Due to this fact, the body of Christ is severing and is in need of a unified restoration. This can be reconciled, however, if we consider the intended meaning behind the Trinity and the union that is offered in it.

The disunity of the church can be restored in the reclaiming of the doctrine of the Trinity and its importance to the Christian church. The Trinity encourages communal living, which keeps the members of the church united. It is clear there are diverse thoughts among traditional churchgoers and the Nones, but if we don't seek unity within our diverse thoughts, then our love is divided. We must come together as a whole and all be willing to listen to one another's baggage as decisions are made to help bring the church back together. I believe the first step is accepting one another's diverse perspectives. This means that we ask each other questions and hear each other out. No matter the presuppositions that are brought to the table, restoration and unity are possible if all parties agree to dialogue in love. We are called to live in community and

2. "Survey," n.p.

to pursue unity. Let us live in the very image that God created us to be, the image that brings about unity within our diversities in the gospel.

## Divisive Love in the Incarnation

One of the primary doctrines in the church is known as the incarnation. This is the physical embodiment of God as he was born of the Virgin Mary. In this embodiment, God took on the very flesh of humanity that we are graced into. According to John C. Clark and Marcus Peter Johnson of the Moody Bible Institute, the incarnation of God is a supreme mystery in which God the Son, without ceasing to be fully God, became fully human.[3] This doctrine is essential in Christian orthodoxy as it depicts the very humanity of Christ Jesus. The incarnation of Christ is crucial for understanding theological anthropology and the importance of bearing God's image. God created humanity in his image and we naturally become the very image-bearers of God. This image was distorted as humanity sinned against God in the Garden of Eden. In Christ, God's broken image-bearers are restored into the very being of who Christ is, and therefore are redeemed into the perfect image of God in Christ. And this is the identity that believers bear as they believe in the gospel by faith.

Today's culture distorts the faithful representation of the incarnation by encouraging a hermeneutic of self-absorption and self-infatuation, which ultimately dishonors the very personhood we ought to model in Christ. Many are consumed with identity and self-image when it comes to finding satisfaction. The image of God is distorted in anything and everything that separates it from the doctrine of the incarnation because it is by and through Christ Jesus we are given our identity. Let us not look any further for who we are in relation to this world apart from Christ alone. Many in the church who disagree with people on how they want to define themselves completely exclude them from their circles.

---

3. Clark and Johnson, *The Incarnation of God*, 11.

The secular world sees Christians as rejecting, unloving, and hateful people. It is important to understand that those in the secular realm who distort the very image of God are indeed sinning against a holy God. But the truth is many in the Christian world are also distorting the image of God by abusing pornography, judging people according to their external looks, and believing their words mean more than a nonbeliever. This is far from the truth. The truth is that both Christians and non-Christians distort the very image of God because both are sinners. The difference is Christians understand their need for the gospel. Yet for some Christians, the transforming power of the gospel does not seem big enough to embrace and love the struggling neighbor who is dealing with identity issues. We would rather choose detrimental behavior than loving our neighbor.

What if instead of divisive love we would choose to love as Christ has first loved us? Perhaps a visual gospel could serve more purpose for the struggling neighbor and produce incredible life-change rather than throat-shoving sermons on how wrong their lifestyle choices are. Have we ever considered how Jesus taught us to treat sinners in the gospels? Jesus emphasized we ought not to judge others, or we too will be judged (Matt 7:1–2). This is especially true if they're nonbelievers because they don't hold to the same standard as those who believe. In the Gospel of John, a woman was caught in adultery and the teachers of the law, along with the Pharisees, brought this woman to Jesus. As they approached the group Jesus was with, they presented this woman and accused her of committing adultery. While doing so, the teachers of the law and the Pharisees began to quote the Torah saying that in it are instructions to stone such a person of misconduct. Along with quoting the Torah, the teachers and Pharisees continued to ask Jesus what he was going to do with her. And Jesus bent over, began drawing in the sand and said, "let any one of you who is without sin be the first to throw a stone at her" (John 8:7). The men had absolutely no verbal response to what Jesus had said, instead they ran away until Jesus was left alone with the woman. Jesus noticed that the teachers and Pharisees were gone and questioned the woman saying, "woman where are they? Has no one condemned you" (John 8:10)? She told him that no one had condemned her, and so Jesus responded that he did not condemn her either. He dismissed her and told her to leave her life of sin.[4]

Too often we choose to treat people as if we have absolutely no baggage ourselves. We bathe in self-righteousness and accuse nonbelievers of being terrible people whose actions are wrong. Perhaps love is not at the forefront of our thinking and instead, we find satisfaction in winning an argument rather than allowing the person to see the true love of Christ. What if we reconsidered the beauty of Christ's incarnation for us? The fact that we too failed God in our broken image-bearing of who he really is? The fact that we sin against the image of God every single day? This is indeed true of both Christians and non-Christians alike, but our hope is in the transforming power of the gospel. Christ bore the very flesh that humanity distorted and transformed it in himself by being a perfect sacrifice for humanity on the cross. This truth redeems all who believe in him. The incarnation of the Son of God gives hope to all who are weary and in need of restoration. Brothers and sisters, let us choose to put on love, which binds us all together in perfect unity, which enables us to be the living gospel to those who need to both see it and hear it.

## Divisive Love in Secondary Issues

This is where love truly divides among Christians. If secondary doctrines are not agreed upon, then one can no longer be part of the work that God is doing within the body of Christ, at least in a certain church body. A love that is divided is not a love that honors God, because it is not love. We have already seen the disunity that occurs even within primary church doctrines. This means that when dealing with secondary issues in the church, disunity will be at the forefront of these issues. Every believer has been

---

4. A paraphrasing of the woman caught in adultery in John 8:1–11.

theologically equipped in their own way. God through the Holy Spirit has placed certain convictions on the hearts of his followers. I want to be clear here when I say this is okay. I also want to make it clear that just because two people have differing views on certain theological positions, does not mean there needs to be a dismantling of a relationship between the people involved. Too often, this is what happens between disagreeing believers. It begins with theological tension, which leads to them using self-defense mechanisms, which is then followed by much argumentation. And those who are extremely passionate about their position or view might even consider pursing disunity. When it comes to the actual church itself, many of our members have differing views on various theological doctrines. As long as we can all agree on the primary doctrines, or the "essentials," I believe it is okay to disagree with one another. The church is filled with people from different theological backgrounds, and we ought to rejoice in this. Why? Because it allows each member of the body to experience something significant that Christ has done in the life of another. After all, no member of the body is exactly the same. How profound would it be to witness the unity of the body, regardless of theological perspective? Consider the following portion of Paul's letter to the church of Corinth:

> Just as a body, though one, has many parts, but all its many parts form one body, so it is with Christ. For we were all baptized by one Spirit so as to form one body—whether Jews or Gentiles, slave or free—and we were all given the one Spirit to drink. Even so the body is not made up of one part but of many.
>
> Now if the foot should say, "Because I am not a hand, I do not belong to the body," it would not for that reason stop being part of the body. And if the ear should say, "Because I am not an eye, I do not belong to the body," it would not for that reason stop being part of the body. If the whole body were an eye, where would the sense of hearing be? If the whole body were an ear, where would the sense of smell be? But in fact God has placed the parts in the body, every one of them, just as he

wanted them to be. If they were all one part, where would the body be? As it is, there are many parts, but one body.

The eye cannot say to the hand, "I don't need you!" And the head cannot say to the feet, "I don't need you!" On the contrary, those parts of the body that seem to be weaker are indispensable, and the parts that we think are less honorable we treat with special honor. And the parts that are unpresentable are treated with special modesty, while our presentable parts need no special treatment. But God has put the body together, giving greater honor to the parts that lacked it, so that there should be no division in the body, but that its parts should have equal concern for each other. If one part suffers, every part suffers with it; if one part is honored, every part rejoices with it.

Now you are the body of Christ, and each one of you is a part of it." (1 Cor 12:12-27, NIV)

We need one another in order to make up the body of Christ. We cannot journey through life alone. This is why despite our theological differences, we are called to become one body in Christ Jesus.

Growing up, I attended a conservative Baptist church. While I attended that church, I knew of many other churches that existed within my geographical location. I also had relationships with people from these various churches, as we would stay connected even though we did not attend the same church. It was interesting when we would gather and talk about other churches because the majority of our conversations revolved around their flaws and shortcomings. To my remembrance, nothing good was ever mentioned. We never discussed how many people were saved in a particular church, rejoicing in God's redemptive work in Christ. We never talked about how incredible the worship experience was. We never addressed the amount of people who wanted to express their response and obedience to the gospel by pursuing baptism. No. We especially focused on the negative things that occurred in those churches, neglecting the work God was doing. Our conversations were filled with words of criticism and hearts of division. Instead of pursuing unity within the church—especially as it related to theological differences—we were completely focused on gossip and the disassembling of the body of believers. The diverse theological convictions of the pastoral leadership were not taken into account as important to us; we simply did not appreciate the various theological conclusions that came about within other churches, as if the eschaton would only consist of those who believed in the same things we affirmed to be proper theology. What was more important to us was division as we pursued the dismantling of the body of Christ, because our theological agenda did not match up with theirs. I get it, we don't have to agree on everything theologically—nor will we—but it is important to remember that all churches have flaws, yet God is doing an incredible work that we cannot lose sight of.

Churches are filled with flaws. If this is a surprise to anyone, welcome to the world we live in. Churches are made up of broken people who are living in a broken world. This means Christians are also imperfect. We talk as if we have it all together and others don't. This type of talk results in further disunity among the body of believers as hearts are hardened and made bitter with gossip. We need to seek God for repentance and ask him to bring about a unifying spirit within out hearts. Only the gospel can break through this depravity that embodies our fallen humanity.

I want to take a minute to reflect on the members' meeting I mentioned earlier in this chapter. I believe what was done there is exactly how the church ought to approach these secondary theological issues. We need to come together, talk, disagree, and ultimately agree to be okay with our differing theological conclusions. Our heart ought to lead us into a thinking that challenges us, the church, and to remain together despite our various theological conclusions. This will bring about unity in the midst of our diverse approaches to our theology. Let's remember the church is called to ultimately put on love, which binds us all together in perfect unity in the gospel of our Lord Jesus Christ (Col 3:14).

I cannot stress enough the importance of the gospel of Christ Jesus. It is this very gospel that is intended to offer love and unity within a diverse church. Jesus Christ came to redeem the sin and hatred in our lives towards one another. When we disagree with one another, oftentimes the intent is to simply win an argument rather than to thoroughly understand the other person. And as the church, our love divides.

## Final Thoughts

We have looked at how the doctrine of the gospel, Trinitarian theology, theology of the incarnation, and secondary-order issues have caused the church to divide. Specifically, that division has occurred in our love towards one another. Due to theological disagreements, churches have looked to have their arguments, win them, and split up. The truth is no one has won any arguments. Repentance is necessary for all in order to be reconciled to Christ. The church is called to love one another as we share in the unity intended in the gospel. God incarnated himself in order to restore human relationships to himself and each other. This very gospel is capable of redeeming the hardened hearts that have neglected many due to various theological disagreements. More often than not, the church is more passionate about dividing over secondary issues than seeking unity in love. So, let us seek to find unity in love rather than pursing division because of our theological differences.

# Chapter 4

# Beautiful Mystery

"Can you fathom the mysteries of God? Can you probe the
limits of the Almighty? They are higher than the heavens
above—what can you do? They are deeper than the depths
below—what can you know? Their measure is longer than the
earth and wider than the sea.

—JOB 11:7–9

MYSTERY IS BEAUTIFUL. JOB knew that. He was constantly experiencing the mysteries of God as he grew closer and deeper in a relationship with God. And Job even recorded truths such as, "Can you fathom the mysteries of God? Can you probe the limits of the Almighty?" (Job 11:7). It is important for us to understand that the God who created the universe is also a beautiful mystery. Even in things that make sense to us regarding our theological understandings, there still remains profound mystery. This is the beauty that is found in God, that God reveals everything humanity needs to know in order to faithfully experience him and his goodness, glory, majesty, power, and love. Yet in the midst of this knowing, one cannot fully comprehend the depths of these things. God is so infinite, that we can only catch a mere glimpse of who he is for us. This is also why God incarnated himself in Christ, so that much of his mystery could be revealed to us, and in knowing Christ, we may know the Father. This is the profound mystery of who God is in Christ Jesus.

It is really easy for Christians to try to limit what God can or cannot do. It is easy to say God is black-and-white in everything. He certainly is when it comes to particular things in the Scriptures, but I think God has left an immense amount of unknowns for us to wrestle with. The reason? So that we may rely upon him more for his glory and to see his purpose fulfilled in our lives. God is mysterious and his mysteries are beautiful. Sanctification (the process of becoming more like God) is the result of the mystery of God because the more we want to know about God, the more we will yearn to seek him in those mysteries. And the more we seek the mysteries of God, the more we will encounter who he truly is.

## Gospel Mystery

The gospel has been made known to us as the way that we may come to know the Father and participate in life everlasting, through the Son of God, Jesus Christ. Yet even in the midst of the understandability of the gospel, there is a multitude of mystery that exists within it. The gospel is scandalous. In his work *Scandalous*, D.A. Carson writes:

> Hear the ironies of the cross: the man who is mocked as king—is king. The man who is utterly powerless—is powerful. The man who can't save Himself—saves others. The man who cries out in despair—trusts God.[1]

Oh how scandalous the mystery of the gospel of Christ Jesus. The very man who was mocked, appeared to be powerless. The very man who wouldn't save Himself from the tortures and pains of bearing the weight of sin, was the man who saved humanity from sin. The very man who cried out in despair to the Father, is the very man who trusted in the Father with every vessel from within. This is Jesus. This is the gospel. And the gospel

1. Carson, *Scandalous*, 36.

is mysterious. We must be okay with the mysteries of the gospel because the gospel saves. It is simple enough to understand for our salvation and perseverance, yet it is complex enough to be mysterious as well scandalous.

The gospel goes beyond the scandal of the cross to prove itself as mysterious. Our tendency and desire to sin mars the very image of God. God is offended by our choice to misrepresent his image by partaking in sin; yet Jesus Christ crushes sin and chooses to represent us before God. This too, is a beautiful mystery. Why would God send his Son into the world for a people that have wronged him by choosing to sin against him (Gen 3)? This is the profound paradoxical reality of God's mystery: his grace is sufficient enough to restore a broken humanity to himself (2 Cor 12:9).

The fact that humanity is willing to choose sin over the riches that are found in Christ is unfathomable. Yet sin has entered into this world—through rebellion and contradiction against God—resulting in our desire and tendency to pursue sin. But where sin increases, grace abounds all the more (Rom 5:20). God created human beings who are the very creatures that bear his image, thus humanity must reflect that glorious and perfect image of God.[2] How tragic it would be if sin was never conquered and destroyed? God, in his sovereign grace, sent his very own Son, Jesus Christ, into the world to be holy and blameless on behalf of all humanity. Christ lived a perfect life on earth and he became sin who knew no sin (2 Cor 5:21). In his perfect life, Christ was the only being in human history who was eligible to be a substitute for sin, on behalf of all humanity. God incarnated himself to live a perfect life on behalf of all humanity, paying the ultimate penalty for sin on the cross at Calvary, and all who believe in him may enjoy everlasting life and the forgiveness of sin. This is the mystery of the gospel. Yet this beautiful mystery has been revealed to those who would incline their ear to hear—and trust in Christ as Lord and Savior—so that the beautiful mystery of the gospel may be known.

Along with this mystery of the gospel comes the mystery of forgiveness. The mystery of forgiveness is we do not deserve to be

---

2. Akin, *A Theology for the Church*, 411.

forgiven—especially by God, Creator of the universe. Why? Because we have rebelled against, wronged, and completely distorted the image of God through the sinful nature we assumed in the fall of man (Gen 3). We constantly choose sin and temptation over the glory and riches of God and his goodness, which has led us to a separation from God. And when we attempt to be better people we end up slipping and falling because we cannot measure up to God and his standards. In order to be reunited in a relationship with God we need to be forgiven for the penalty of sin. What's important to understand is we do not deserve forgiveness, yet God in his mercy and grace offers forgiveness to all who confess their sins, believe Jesus Christ is Lord and Savior, and believe God raised him from the dead, giving us hope and new life (Rom 10:9). Why God would do this freely for us, yet at such a high cost in sacrificing his Son on the cross, is unfathomable. But this is the beautiful mystery of God: that we are undeserving of his love, but he still chooses to pursue us and forgive us because God is love (1 John 4:8). So rest in this profound love of God that is found in the birth, life, ministry, death, resurrection, and ascension of Christ Jesus, who is our Lord.

## Trinitarian Mystery

The Trinity is a doctrine that has been disagreed upon throughout the history of the church, mainly because it was affiliated with countless heresies in early Christianity. Church historians have disagreed on the doctrine of the Trinity because it was extremely complex to comprehend, thus conclusions were assumed and heresies were brought forth. The reason many heresies came about regarding the Trinity is because Scripture does not explicitly teach a Trinitarian view of God,[3] although the Scripture does teach that God is one and that three persons are God, thus affirming the doctrine of the Trinity.[4] Therefore the Trinity is affirmed in the

---

3. Erickson, *Christian Theology*, 291.
4. Ibid, 291.

Scriptures—yet the triunity of God is never explicitly mentioned. What a beautiful mystery that is found in the Godhead of the Father, Son, and Holy Spirit. God remains mysterious in the ways he works, communicates, loves, and forgives, in order for us to encounter his triune nature.

The doctrine of the Trinity conveys mystery, as many have attempted to explain the Trinity through analogies. This is the result of the Trinity not being seen as a solution and delight, but rather an oddity and a problem.[5] For instance, Michael Reeves articulates:

> Think, for example, of all those desperate-sounding illustrations. "The Trinity," some helpful soul explains, "is like an egg, where there is the shell, the yolk and the white, and yet it is all one egg!" "No," says another, "the Trinity is more like a shamrock leaf: that's one leaf, but it's got three bits sticking out. *Just* like the Father, Son, and Spirit." And one wonders why the world laughs. For whether the Trinity is compared to shrubbery, streaky bacon, the three states of H2O or a three-headed giant, it begins to sound, well, bizarre, like some pointless and unsightly growth on our understanding of God, one that could surely be lopped off with no consequence other than a universal sigh of relief.[6]

These perceptions of the Trinity are what distort the beautiful mystery of who God is. We cannot attempt to explain in mere human words why the Trinity works, even though through the revelation of the Holy Spirit believers are able to comprehend these depths (at times). Analogies aren't always helpful, even though we want them to be. God is mysterious, and in his mystery he is triune.

It is because the Trinity is such a beautiful mystery of God expressing himself to humanity through his trinitarian nature that we can dwell on the profound mysteries of God and who he is for mankind. God is not like an egg, nor is God like a shamrock leaf. God is the Trinity—Father, Son, and Holy Spirit—the embodiment

5. Reeves, *Delighting in the Trinity*, 10.
6. Ibid, 10.

of a beautiful mystery of community and relationship. This is a beautiful mystery, and humanity—bearing the very *imago Dei*, or image of God—we ought to manifest this very representation of community and relationship with one another in the body of Christ. A beautiful symbol of oneness, just as God intended. The Trinity serves to nourish the believer in oneness so the bride of Christ may abound in the deepest love and affection, bringing forth unity in the gospel.

## Incarnational Mystery

The doctrine of the incarnation is yet another beautiful mystery. This doctrine, at times, proves to be controversial. The reason for this controversy is skeptics find it hard to believe that the creator God would be born of a virgin in order to become man so he could live a perfect, sinless life, reconciling humanity back to himself. J.I. Packer said it best, "It is no wonder that thoughtful people find the gospel of Jesus Christ hard to believe, for the realities with which it deals pass our understanding."[7] Packer acknowledges that the beautiful mysteries of God indeed surpass all understanding. God, in his mysterious nature, entered into our humanity in the form of a sinless being who would change the world forever. Jesus Christ, the Son of God, assumed the very humanity you and I bear. He assumed the very flesh and blood we are made up of. Yet unlike sinful humanity, this perfect Savior lived without sin. Jesus experienced temptation (Matt 4:1–11), exhaustion (John 4:6), sorrow (John 11:35), and pain and suffering (Luke 22:63–65), among many other things humanity faces. This is because Jesus Christ was fully man and fully God (Heb 2:14). The very human nature that Christ possessed, we possess. Although, what separates us from Christ is that Christ was perfect in his humanness. At the same time, Christ was fully God (Col 2:9), and this is the profound mystery of the incarnation: that Jesus Christ experienced everything a human

---

7. Packer, *Knowing God*, 52.

being experiences, yet he did so without sinning as he became sin on the cross for the redemption of all who believe in him.

What a mystery that God would come down into the trenches of earth and its sin in order to restore humanity to himself through a loving, eternal relationship with his children. This had to be done in order for God to restore our relationship with him, and this beautiful mystery has been revealed to us in God's actions of bearing flesh and blood. It is through this flesh and blood that we acquire salvation and union with Christ Jesus, who is our Lord. Salvation unites us into the very oneness that is shared between the Father, Son, and Holy Spirit, and thus we too must share in this oneness together, allowing us to sacrifice ourselves for the body of Christ. In this, we will grow in unity, which will better resemble the incarnation of Christ and his love for humanity so that pursuing God's love may become our main objective.

## Secondary Issues and Mystery

The truth is God is mysterious. We have just covered the beautiful mystery of God in the gospel of Christ, his triune nature, and the incarnation of God in Christ Jesus. These key doctrines hold the Christian faith together and many derive other doctrines from them which are relevant and crucial for the church and its foundation. Yet when it comes to secondary issues in the church, many of these areas remain gray. Let me explain.

If *everything* is clear in the Bible, then why are there countless views on the atonement of Jesus Christ? Why are there countless views on justification in biblical scholarship? Why do we have so many articulations of what the end times will look like, yet no one truly knows for sure? Only assumptions can be made. Why is the Lord's Supper taken in so many different ways as many believe very different things about the significance of the elements? Why do we have so many views on atonement theory and the person and work of Christ, if God is black-and-white? Why does the role of the Holy Spirit differ depending on which denomination one comes from? I believe these conversations exist because God has not revealed every single detail to us regarding our lives and himself, yet he has revealed the mysteries of his grand narrative of redemption and restoration so we may know who he is through the gospel of his Son, Jesus Christ.

We can disagree on the beautiful mysteries of who God is and how he wants our churches to function, but what is at the core of these disagreements? Is it pride? Selfishness? Insecurity? A desire to have it all right? I strongly believe many of us may be close to getting some things right, but if we are honest with ourselves we may actually be wrong about many things. But who wants to admit that? Do we dare show our weaknesses with the body of Christ? Love remains as the key to uniting our churches theologically, to bring God glory and to unify his children in love.

Think for a moment like a parent. Does a parent desire their children to fight all the time so that disunity of relationships occurs in the future? Or does a parent attempt to mediate their children in the midst of chaos, disagreements, and selfishness in order to unite the family? I think it is the latter, and perhaps you do too. We were made for something more than tearing each other apart over the mysteries of secondary theological issues. We were made to embrace one another in Christ, with love, so the church may become one, as intended by Christ himself. Hear the *emotion* and *desire* of Christ as he prays for all believers:

> My prayer is not for them alone. I pray also for those who will believe in me through their message, that all of them may be one, Father, just as you are in me and I am in you. May they also be in us so that the world may believe that you have sent me. I have given them the glory that you gave me, that they may be one as we are one—I in them and you in me—so that they may be brought to complete unity. Then the world will know that you sent me and have loved them even as you have loved me. Father, I want those you have given me to be with me where I am, and to see my glory, the glory you have given me because you loved me before the creation of the world. Righteous Father, though the world does not know you, I know you, and they know that you have sent me. I have made you

known to them, and will continue to make you known in order that the love you have for me may be in them and that I myself may be in them. (John 17:20–26)

Allow this prayer of Jesus to dwell within you, searching his desires for his children to dwell in oneness and unity, just as the Father, Son, and Holy Spirit do.

## Beautiful Mystery

If we think we have figured God out, then we have it all wrong. God is unfathomable. He was never meant to be figured out. God gave us all we need in order to enjoy him, experience him, and in order for us to have a relationship with him through the salvation that is offered in his Son, Jesus Christ. He has revealed many other things about himself to us so we may know who our heavenly Father is, but God cannot be fully understood as there are many mysteries he possesses. The world is a complex place, and if that is the case then we must acknowledge that God himself is complex. This is not something that should worry us; rather, it ought to be something that draws us more towards a posture of awe and worship. There are just some things we cannot comprehend when we think about who God is; thus, being content with mystery is actually glorifying to God. When we embrace the reality that God is mysterious, we can experience him in a profound way through our deep reverence for his character. Receiving God as mysterious takes on a posture of humility, which seeks to embrace his very mysteries as beautiful. But often we tend to fear being in the unknown as we attempt to develop answers regarding theological concepts. When we endeavor upon this journey we risk the mysteries of God as paradox, ultimately leading to stiff theological presumptions. This creates a heart of having it all together theologically, ultimately leading to division amongst believers through disagreements instead of being content with mystery.

Many theologians seem to have all the answers, and if they're disagreed with they will retaliate as if you had started war on their territory. How dare we intrude on each others' theological frameworks! This gives birth to disunity and leads to many disagreements, which more often than not end in the severing of relationships. I have personally seen this occur amongst believers (and was certainly an advocate of disunity myself), but there comes a time when these silly arguments must come to an end. If we are not intending to *edify* and *unite* the body of Christ in our theological disagreements, then we are wasting the breath that was so freely given to us by the grace of God. As the church, let us acknowledge that our eternal Creator has made a world filled with mystery, as he himself is mysterious.

God is forever immortal and bestows infinite mystery. He has made himself known to us in Christ Jesus. When Paul wrote his epistle to the Colossians, he eagerly sought to inform the church of his passion for unity in love (Col 2:1–2). In this plea for unity in love, Paul urges that the full riches of complete understanding will come about, in order that the church may understand the mystery of God, namely Christ (Col 2:2). Paul goes on to address that this Christ is the one in whom are hidden the treasures of wisdom and knowledge (Col 2:3), meaning that in Christ Jesus, we experience the beautiful mysteries that exist. God has made himself known in his Son Jesus Christ so the mysteries of God may be understood in him. But what God has revealed to us is the mystery of the gospel of Jesus Christ. Paul writes to the Colossians:

> I have become its servant by the commission God gave me to present to you the word of God in its fullness—the mystery that has been kept hidden for ages and generations, but is now disclosed to the Lord's people. To them God has chosen to make known among the Gentiles the glorious riches of this mystery, which is Christ in you, the hope of glory. (Col 1:25–27)

The mystery of the gospel has been revealed, and this mystery forever changes those who believe so they may experience the goodness of God's love for them. The gospel reveals a new command which is to love God, and to love others (Mark 12:30–31). What a mystery that God would send his one and only Son for us!

Yet this mystery is revealed through God's love for his creation. Let us rejoice in the beautiful mystery of who Christ is for us.

# Chapter 5

# Where Do We Go from Here?

*I appeal to you, brothers and sisters, in the name of our Lord Jesus Christ, that all of you agree with one another in what you say and that there be no divisions among you, but that you be perfectly united in mind and thought.*

—1 CORINTHIANS 1:10

THE JOURNEY WE HAVE been on in our attempt to establish unity within a theologically diverse church does not end here. We need to ask ourselves: "Where do we go from here?" In this final chapter, I will attempt to bring about a few practical challenges for the church that is in pursuit of unity despite differing theological opinions.

In the previous four chapters we have covered the purpose of studying theology and its importance to our faith, as well as the implications and importance of studying theology. We have looked at some primary doctrines that define the Christian faith, and help us understand who God really is. We have also discussed some of the doctrines (secondary-order issues) which can be controversial in the church, thus causing division among believers with varying perspectives. We have looked at how our love for one another in Christ can be divided through our disagreements about diverse theological opinions that exist in the church. In the previous chapter we addressed the mysteries of God, as well as understanding that God himself is a beautiful mystery.

It seems as if God is not black-and-white when it comes to many secondary theological issues, thus explaining why the church at large comes to many conclusions on what they perceive to be true theologically. It is because not everything is made clear, because God is mysterious. And we need to be okay with this fact. God intended for humanity to know many things, but he also intended for us not to know everything, hence the garden of Eden. God created all things good. He intended for humanity to flourish in his presence and in his creation. He made everything known that needed to be known, providing all things necessary for the sustainability of life. In the midst of his creation, God created a tree whose fruit produced the knowledge of good and evil (Gen 2:9), and humanity became determined to know more than God had intended. This resulted in the fall of humanity, as humanity sought to know more than was needed. It is untrue that we cannot pursue knowing the things of God, but I do think it is important to realize we will not all get it right. God is mysterious and has not revealed all things doctrinal. God has indeed revealed all things gospel, as this is paramount for our salvation and our knowing the Lord Jesus. God has revealed trinitarianism to us so we may know his very nature, as well as who he is in relation to us, his creation. God has also revealed the incarnation to us so we may know that the Son of God, Jesus Christ, took upon himself the very nature of who we are (flesh and bone) and paid the penalty for our sin on the cross so we may have life everlasting. The rest is for us to be as faithful as possible, bringing about our various doctrines for the sustenance of the church.

## Understanding Presuppositions

Every single person comes from a different cultural background and a different upbringing with respect to understanding theological concepts. This doesn't mean certain people are wrong, it just means their perspective is different from yours or mine. Every single person that frames a theological perspective comes from a presupposition of some sort. John Wesley developed a system which was later coined as the "Wesleyan Quadrilateral" by Albert C. Outler. The Wesleyan Quadrilateral was established to determined how doctrinal conclusions came about. According to Outler, the Wesleyan Quadrilateral included Scripture, tradition, reason, and experience.[1] These four approaches to our theology, develop our understanding.

Every doctrinal conclusion stems from Scripture in one way or another, because apart from Scripture we cannot assume a doctrine is accurate. As we approach the various second-order issues within the church, we see that each argument incorporates Scripture in some form. After scriptural defense for a theological position, tradition plays an important part in one's theological influence. We all grow up with various traditions which influence the kind of people we become. Many traditions are upheld by the individual as they grow up, but for others, traditions become a thing of the past. Many are influenced theologically based on particular traditions. Some may affirm theological perspectives based on what church fathers believed and wrote about. This holds fast to church history and its tradition, as it unfolds within our theological understandings today. For others, interpretations may come about from the tradition of upbringing and familial context.

Growing up, church was a chore. It was something I absolutely could not stand attending. The reason for this is church was boring and everyone seemed to have it all together. People were always wearing nice clothing, appearing to be very proper, and seeming to have life figured out. I knew I did not fit in with these people because I certainly did not have it all together. This church was rooted in fundamentalism and exemplified a very traditional approach to church. This pushed me away from the church to the point where I decided to give up on church because I simply could not measure up to the standards of the church. By God's grace, I was eventually able to get back to church, but this time around my views and perspectives on the church had shifted. In fact, the way

1. Outler. "The Wesleyan Quadrilateral in Wesley," 7–9.

I was used to church did not even exist in my ecclesial framework. I looked at my first church as an example of how *not* do church. The point is my tradition and upbringing had shaped the way I understood theology in regards to the church. The baggage I had accumulated in my childhood church forced me to develop a theology that contradicted fundamentalism. Am I right in that way of thinking? Absolutely not. The fundamentalist church has its good parts and no church is perfect, but this was not for me. The reality is my tradition and upbringing influenced my understanding of church. In other words, my theology of the church was formed from bad experiences in the church.

My experiences in the fundamentalist church negatively affected my understanding of church as a whole. Experience is another leg of the Wesleyan Quadrilateral. Every single person comes from a multitude of experiences that shape who they become, and in a book about theological diversity, we must pose the question: "How have my experiences shaped my theology?" Some, like me, have come from a background of fundamentalism. Others grew up in the Catholic Church. Some never saw the inside of a church until recently. Would these experiences shape our theologies in completely different ways? Absolutely. Yet for some reason, we neglect the truth that experience is essential to our theological development. The reason theological diversity exists is because we have all come from varying life experiences which shape the way we think about God. Again, we may see things differently in many theological understandings, but the goal is to have the conversation with one another in love.

Finally, reason is another leg in the Wesleyan Quadrilateral. We must understand that many people come to their theological conclusions based on reason. Scripture certainly is all-sufficient and provides many of the answers we need theologically, yet reason, according to Wesley, allows us to understand the essential truths about Scripture. Wesley has a distinctive theological method for understanding the interpretation of the text:

> With Scripture as its preeminent norm but interfaced with tradition, reason and Christian experience as dynamic and interactive aids in the interpretation of the

Word of God in Scripture. Such a method takes it for granted that faith is human re-action to an antecedent action of the Holy Spirit's prevenience, aimed at convicting our consciences and opening our eyes and ears to God's address to us in Scripture. This means that our "knowledge of God and of the things of God" is more nearly a response of trusting faith in God in Christ as Grace Incarnate than it is a mental assent to dogmatic formulations however true.[2]

Wesley is articulating that Scripture indeed is the preeminent and most important way in bringing about biblical interpretation, yet tradition, reason, and Christian experience are dynamic and interactive aids for our biblical interpretation. Thus many who approach the text approach it with a posture of tradition, a posture of reason, and a posture of experience. It is important to incorporate the varying reactions Christians may have regarding the Holy Spirit's convictions in their lives. The point is many come to different conclusions theologically and the goal is not to point fingers while letting tempers flare; rather, the goal is to pursue gospel unity for God's final end, which is love.

When making theological conclusions and assumptions, it is important to consider the Wesleyan Quadrilateral as a useful resource in understanding the variety of theologies that exist. Many have been influenced by Scripture, yes, but many have come to interpret Scripture from their traditions. Others have interpreted the Scripture from the context of personal experience (which cannot be overlooked), as a basis for understanding certain Scriptures. Lastly, many interpret Scripture based on reason, which ultimately develops the multitude of theological understandings that exist. Because of these conclusions, many Christian denominations exist.

## Purpose of Denominations

It is interesting that Christianity is filled with a vast array of denominations which all hold to significant doctrinal differences.

2. Outler. "The Wesleyan Quadrilateral in Wesley," 9.

The question that lies at hand is: "Which denominational doctrine is correct and which is incorrect?" Who is to say one is right and the other is wrong? All denominations use the Bible as a source for determining truth, but many of us come to a handful of conclusions theologically. One would think that if God indeed was black-and-white regarding secondary-order issues, we would all come to the same conclusions. But the reality is we don't. And the question remains, who is correct? Taking Wesley's idea of the quadrilateral, we see that our theological ideologies stem from our upbringing. Perhaps we cling to a particular denomination because we were brought up in that denomination, so those theological perspectives may be all we know when it comes to our thinking about God. Perhaps when some read the Scriptures, they see things as clear and develop theological conclusions based on what they presume to be accurate.

I have been in too many Bible studies where people have been asked to read a passage and then share what it means to them. This is one of the most fascinating exercises for me because I know once people begin talking, there will be multitudes of interpretations of any particular text. It is rather entertaining to hear how each person perceives the text being discussed, not from a theological student's perspective, but from the perspective of understanding one's presuppositional and (previous) denominational perspective. Each individual has a unique contribution to the discussion when it comes to what the Holy Spirit is teaching him or her, but when someone is completely immersed in their theological framework, there may be a dismissal of another's comment or statement regarding the text. It is important to have views and perspectives while holding to sound doctrine, but it is also important to not dismiss others immediately, because their theological presuppositions stem from a denominational upbringing.

## Heart Change

When I first became a believer, I was really passionate and excited to get things right in my faith. I wanted to learn everything about the Bible and theology. I would say that a few years into studying theology, I became pretty snarky. I was sure I figured everything out. I was a five-point Calvinist, reformed, and there was nothing outside of my understanding of proper theology.

I urge everyone who is reading this book to consider a heart change. I don't mean that we drop all of our theological and doctrinal convictions out the window. In fact, I believe we ought to fully hold fast to what we truly believe the Lord is convicting us of. But for those who have been side-swiped by dogmatic tendencies, I especially want to challenge you to consider a heart change. This plea is not to remove your doctrinal thinking and understanding; rather, this plea is to open our hearts with a vulnerable approach to the Spirit of God, as we allow diverse theological ideologies to be considered within our thinking.

## Gray Theology

Theological diversity exists as a passion for me and I would classify theological diversity as *gray* theology. We can refer to things or ideas as not being black-and-white, but I would argue God himself is not black-and-white or clear about *every single* theological concept. Let me explain. I believe God imself is omniscient (all-knowing), but we are not. God is omnipotent (all-powerful), but we are not. God is omnipresent (all-present), and we are not. The point is this: God knows everything and we do not. Often, we try and figure God out as if studying about him for a long time suggests we have figured him out. God has chosen not to reveal every single thing for us to know, thus explaining why many things in Christian theology are a mystery, and this mystery is indeed beautiful. The God of the universe has chosen to reveal the most incredible gift to us—Jesus Christ. God has revealed Jesus Christ so we may fully experience and understand the love of God for his people. This is done through the sacrificial and sovereign love of God for humanity. What would life be like if we lived out this kind of love towards one another? Would we continue to dispute theologically for the sake of winning an argument, seeking to be right? Or, would we allow the love demonstrated in the gospel to transform us and make us new?

Gray theology exists because we do not have answers for everything. Many of us are not okay with that reality because we want to come across as if we know it all. Trust me, I've been there, and this is why I have been eager to write this book. I believe everyone who is stuck in their dogma should consider gray theology, a way of thinking which welcomes loving conversations regarding theology. Perhaps the Spirit of the living God, the same Spirit that raised Christ from the grave, may change a prideful and dogmatic heart, which will bring about vulnerability and love for God's people.

## Where Do We Go from Here?

It is important for our churches to seek unity regardless of theological diversity so we may be made whole in Christ Jesus, rather than allowing our disagreements to lead into church division and splitting. Every church has a different understanding of the theological dynamics of how the local church should gather, function, be governed, and carry out missions, and vast perspectives on the Bible and its interpretation. These varying interpretations for churches could be based on presuppositions that have been ushered into the congregation. These interpretations could be rooted in the church's upbringing, whether it be via the pastoral staff, elder board, or church heritage. Others may be rooted in cultural context. Perhaps people's perspectives are driven by the way their culture has always approached certain aspects of theology. But for the most part, these truths are not taken into consideration when dialoguing about theological perspectives. Many go into a theological conversation looking to prove someone else wrong for the sake of pride. This is exactly how I used to live, and I noticed the bitterness that was welling up from within towards those who did not see things the way I did. What if I at least gave others a chance to explain how and why they arrived at certain conclusions theologically? I believe the church would be a better place if we had these conversations, rather than dismissing one another out of the desire to win an argument, to feel as though we are right and someone else is wrong. The sad reality is oftentimes this is indeed the case. Let us fix our eyes on the gospel of Christ Jesus, which compels us to live our lives in unity with one another.

There is a reason there is an abundance of theological conclusions regarding secondary-order issues. Not only that, there are numerous perspectives within the primary theological issues as well. Simply put, all aspects of theology bring about some sort of controversial dialogue. I believe it is our duty—those who are in the church—to partake in loving, gospel-centered dialogue about our varying theological perspectives, hearing each other out for the glory of God. I've been around too many critics to know that some people are completely close-minded to theological diversity, robbing the Spirit of the work that can be done in one's heart. I am simply urging for those who are in the church to hear one another out in various theological conclusions while maintaining a heart of openness and love.

## Final Thoughts

I want to be clear and articulate that I am not saying we should not have doctrinal convictions in our approaches of doing and studying theology. Everyone ought to hold fast to their convictions, as they are from God. If a particular church has their primary doctrines in tact and has a set of secondary doctrines which define what the church believes, to God be the glory. The purpose of this book is not to negate the importance of the various doctrines that exist in the church. In fact, there are things I believe are second-order issues which I firmly believe the Scriptures teach. Some of those doctrines would be disagreed upon by many of my peers, and that is okay. My push is for a conversation. A conversation that brings about unity between those who often disagree amongst one another. A conversation where two or more can gather and partake in, which is filled with differing perspectives regarding theological methods, approaches, and conclusions, yet they hear one another out on why certain conclusions have been reached.

And at the end of the conversation, no one's intention is to change the other's thinking—rather, it is to simply engage in dialogue that produces fruit and edification for the glory of God and the body of Christ.

Instead of always trying to win an argument with our peers using phrases like, "the Bible says . . .," we ought to focus on the new covenant which is found in Christ Jesus. The Bible says many things in regards to theology and affirms different theological conclusions. Some of which may even contradict themselves. But this should not be our focus. Instead, our focus ought to be on Christ and his new covenant. This covenant is to love God and others (Mark 12:30–31). When we disagree with others, we must ask ourselves: "How did Jesus treat people?" He treated them with love. Love must be at the epicenter of our intentions in every circumstance that comes our way. Our goal should not be division, but instead we must pursue unity within the very power of love that is found in the gospel.

It is easy to live believing we're right about everything while everyone else who doesn't see God the way we do must be completely out of touch with their theology. Let us not be stuck in our dogmatic thinking, which can often harden our hearts to the things the Holy Spirit can change within us. If this becomes our identity, then we have missed the whole point of being sensitive to the Spirit's guidance and leading as we mature and persevere in our faith. Would we ever consider being open and willing to receiving one's theological assumptions based on their context and upbringing? Would we dare consider having a conversation without always being ready to load our theological rifles and shoot our dogma at the other party? I believe God can do an incredible work in the hearts of all believers in order to bring the body of Christ together again, where it was intended to be since the beginning of the church in Acts. Luke wrote:

> They devoted themselves to the apostles' teaching and to fellowship, to the breaking of bread and to prayer. Everyone was filled with awe at the many wonders and signs performed by the apostles. All the believers were

together and had everything in common. They sold property and possessions to give to anyone who had need. Every day they continued to meet together in the temple courts. They broke bread in their homes and ate together with glad and sincere hearts, praising God and enjoying the favor of all the people. And the Lord added to their number daily those who were being saved. (Acts 2:42–47)

Brothers and sisters, this is exactly how the church of Jesus Christ ought to display herself among other believers, nonbelievers, and broken and hurt believers. We ought to devote ourselves to the teaching and fellowship of the apostles' teaching, which was always rooted in the gospel of Christ Jesus, the Savior of the world. We ought to break bread as a symbol of unity in Christ as we praise Him through our prayers in adoration, thanksgiving, confession, and supplication. We must pursue unity within one another as we share in the reality of what the gospel has done for us and what the gospel continues to do in and through us. We must share with one another all that has been given to us by the mercy and grace of God as we praise God, while enjoying his people. His people are our community and as a community of believers we must share our lives with one another in love. By doing so, many will see what the gospel does in the hearts of the people of God, and God in his faithfulness will multiply his kingdom. So let us proclaim the good news of Jesus Christ and seek to be faithful to the gospel, which encourages love and unity within the body of Christ and his people.

My hope is the conversation does not end here; rather, I hope this book begins turning the wheels towards the important conversation in the church regarding unity in the gospel. The body of Christ at large does not need to be another victim of division, which shatters relationships based on theological disagreements, causing broken relationships, a heavy dose of pride, and a serious tendency to gossip. No, we need to be a church that resembles the very gospel of Jesus Christ which brings about love, joy, peace, sacrifice, and unity, because the reality is people are tired of hypocrisy, judgment, condemnation, shaming, etc., and the church, sadly, is very good at displaying these traits to many who enter through their doors. Rather, we need to share one another's burdens in and through the love of the gospel, and it all starts with realizing that God is not black-and-white when it comes to every theological understanding. How much different would the church look if we came together in the gospel, allowing Christ to bring unity within our theological diversity, for the glory of God and his kingdom work and purpose?

# Conclusion

BROTHERS AND SISTERS, MY passion and intent for this book rests in bringing unity to the body of believers, who so often value uniformity on secondary doctrinal issues. Instead, we must give way for the gospel of Jesus Christ—which is love—to cause us to embrace secondary issues as something we can agree to disagree on. Let us hold fast to that which is primary, that which defines the very faith which we profess. How can we disagree upon what the gospel of Christ means to us? This is what our very faith affirms. Whether Catholic, Presbyterian, Lutheran, Baptist, Methodist, Anabaptist, Pentecostal, Seventh-Day Adventist, Orthodox, Non-Denominational, or fill in your blank, we can all agree that Jesus Christ, the Second Person of the Trinity, incarnated himself and lived a perfect life in order to restore humanity from their rebellious and sinful nature. In this restoration, Christ bore the very sins we commit upon himself, sacrificing his life on the cross at Calvary so we may eternally live in him. We can also agree that God is three persons, yet assumes one nature. This is who God is, and in affirming God as God, we affirm that he is Father, Son, and Holy Spirit. Finally, God incarnated himself into the very flesh and blood we possess. In doing so, he became fully man, lived a perfect life, and took up the cross in order to pay the penalty for our sin.

Even if we continue to disagree on secondary doctrinal issues, we ought to at least consider a love-oriented dialogue about why we believe what we believe so the body of Christ may pursue oneness through the gospel. In a new command that was given by Jesus to his disciples on the night of the Last Supper, Christ strongly urged them to "Love one another. As I have loved you, so you must love one another. By this everyone will know that you are my disciples, if you love one another" (John 13:34–35). We must model ourselves as the children of God, in love, so all may know we are in Christ Jesus. Just as Jesus taught his disciples, we are called to love one another, and by this we will be known as Christ-followers.

Secondary doctrinal conversations and praxes are very important. Both primary and secondary doctrines are crucial, functioning components of every church. But what if rather than relying so heavily on secondary-order issues, we took the approach of the gospel? What if we embraced people for who they are in the eyes of Christ Jesus our Lord, rather than a category of theological thought? Why address people as "Calvinists" or "Arminians," when we can refer to each other as followers of Christ instead? Again, secondary doctrines are very important, and so are the nuances of denominations, but our faith has more substance than merely our stance on secondary theological issues. Because secondary doctrines are so important, let us consider allowing Christians with all sorts of perspectives and views on secondary issues to have open dialogue with the purpose of loving one another.

## Secondary Issues and Confusion?

Often we act as if we have got it all figured out theologically. We come to conclusions about theological perspectives, but yet when further study is done many people see things in many ways. So who's got it figured out? You? Me? Or is God not black-and-white when it comes to secondary issues? Because if he was indeed black-and-white we would not have five-plus views on every theological issue. Instead, we would have *one stance* since every church would agree about *everything* theologically, because "God is clear about it . . ." Right? Think about this: The way we think about how we are justified in Christ does not change the fact that we are justified in Christ. How we perceive the atonement does not change the fact that the atonement took place as we acquire the benefits of it. Our view of the end times (eschatology) does not change what God's plans are for the eschaton as he will do whatever he wills. We are merely playing a guessing game, supporting it with Scripture, and coming to our theological conclusions. That is not wrong at all. In fact, it is exactly what we are supposed to do: discern all of our theological conclusions with Scripture. But then we dialogue with one another in the church, and various conclusions come about from what we think the biblical text is articulating. We do contextual work, historical work, and serious biblical study, yet still fall short of seeing things exactly the same. Why? Because God is not black-and-white about everything we want to believe, yet truth rests in the fact that we ought to seek unity in a theologically diverse church. And this is achieved through the gospel of Christ Jesus, which unites believers in love, bringing about unity within our diversities.

Let us have conversations regarding second-order doctrinal issues and let us allow these conversations to mold us into the image of Christ's bride—the church—the way he intended. Let's allow these conversations to knit us together in unity, as intended by Christ, even if we come to varying conclusions theologically. Let us develop a posture of iron-sharpening and sanctification, rather than a posture of baggage and dysfunction because disunity in the church is the exact opposite of what Christ proclaimed in his earthly ministry. He proclaimed unity within the body of believers to the point that he united himself with those who believe in him so we may have direct access to God the Father Almighty. Christ cares for his bride. He sanctifies his bride, ultimately seeking a beautiful and mysterious union with his bride, the church.

So how will we respond? How will we allow Christ Jesus to use us in the midst of our current situation theologically? Will we allow the Holy Spirit to mold and shape us into the image of Christ? Or, will division continue to reign as the primary focus of our theology?

As you go, I highly encourage you to ponder and meditate upon the verses provided at the end. Take time to deeply study the Scriptures (especially the ones provided below), knowing that God will speak to you in their profound tone. Rely on the Holy Spirit to speak to you in light of the church at large. We are God's children, and he does not desire us to neglect one another, even in our differences, because we are all uniquely created as we await the return of our Savior.

I pray this book was helpful in addressing the common issue of disunity within the body of Christ. Let us strive to pursue unity in the church as we anticipate Christ showing up in our midst. One day, we will all dwell together in paradise, participating in the unity that is found in the gospel, which is the love of Christ Jesus for those who believe and trust in him.

# Biblical Texts for Further Study on Unity

I appeal to you, brothers and sisters, in the name of our Lord Jesus Christ, that all of you agree with one another in what you say and that there be no divisions among you, but that you be perfectly united in mind and thought.

—1 CORINTHIANS 1:10

So Christ himself gave the apostles, the prophets, the evangelists, the pastors and teachers, to equip his people for works of service, so that the body of Christ may be built up until we all reach unity in the faith and in the knowledge of the Son of God and become mature, attaining to the whole measure of the fullness of Christ.

—EPHESIANS 4:11–13

Bear with each other and forgive one another if any of you has a grievance against someone. Forgive as the Lord forgave you. And over all these virtues put on love, which binds them all together in perfect unity.

—COLOSSIANS 3:13–14

I in them and you in me—so that they may be brought to complete unity. Then the world will know that you sent me and have loved them even as you have loved me.

—JOHN 17:23

How good and pleasant it is when God's people live together in unity!

—PSALM 133:1

Finally, all of you, be like-minded, be sympathetic, love one another, be compassionate and humble.

—1 PETER 3:8

No one has ever seen God; but if we love one another, God lives in us and his love is made

complete in us.

—1 JOHN 4:12

## God is not Black-and-White

So in Christ Jesus you are all children of God through faith, for all of you who were baptized into Christ have clothed yourselves with Christ. There is neither Jew nor Gentile, neither slave nor free, nor is there male and female, for you are all one in Christ Jesus.

—GALATIANS 3:26–28

# Bibliography

Akin, L. Daniel. *A Theology for the Church*. Nashville: B&H, 2007.

Allison, Gregg R. *Sojourners and Strangers: The Doctrine of the Church*. Edited by John S. Feinberg. Foundations of Evangelical Theology. Wheaton, IL: Crossway, 2012.

"Apostles' Creed," https://www.crcna.org/welcome/beliefs/creeds/apostles-creed.

Calvin, John. *Institutes of the Christian Religion*. Rev. ed. Peabody, MA: Hendrickson, 2007.

Carson, D. A. *Scandalous: The Cross and Resurrection of Jesus*. Wheaton, IL: Crossway, 2010.

Clark, John, and Marcus Peter Johnson. *The Incarnation of God: The Mystery of the Gospel as the Foundation of Evangelical Theology*. Wheaton, IL: Crossway, 2015.

Engle, Paul E., et al. *Understanding Four Views on the Lord's Supper*. Edited by John H. Armstrong. Grand Rapids: Zondervan, 2007.

Erickson, Millard J., *Christian Theology*, 3rd ed. Grand Rapids: Baker Academic, 2013.

Gros, Jeffrey, et al. *Introduction to Ecumenism*. New York: Paulist, 1998.

Lewis, C.S., *Mere Christianity*. Rev. ed. New York: Harper Collins, 2009.

McKnight, Scot. *The Blue Parakeet: Rethinking How You Read the Bible*. Grand Rapids: Zondervan, 2010.

Nichols, Stephen J. *Martin Luther: A Guided Tour of His Life and Thought*. Phillipsburg, NJ: P & R, 2002.

Nichols, Terence. "Transubstantiation and Eucharistic Presence," *Pro Ecclesia* 11, no. 1 (2002) 57-75.

Outler, C. Albert. "The Wesleyan Quadrilateral in John Wesley," *Wesleyan Theological Journal* 20.1 (1985) 7-18.

# Bibliography

Packer, J.I. *Knowing God.* 20th anniversary edition. Downers Grove, IL: IVP, 1993.

Reeves, Michael. *Delighting in the Trinity: An Introduction to the Christian Faith.* Downers Grove, IL: IVP Academic, 2012.

Sproul, R. C. *What Is the Trinity?* 10. The Crucial Questions Series. Orlando: Reformation Trust, 2011.

"Survey: U.S. Church Attendance Sinks to Record Low, but Prayer Is Still Resilient in the Age of the Nones." http://www.patheos.com/blogs/friendlyatheist/2015/03/08/survey-u-s-church-attendance-sinks-to-record-low-but-prayer-is-still-resilient-in-the-age-of-the-nones/.

Vander Zee, Leonard J. *Christ, Baptism, and the Lord's Supper: Recovering the Sacraments for Evangelical Worship.* Downers Grove, IL: InterVarsity, 2004.

# Author Index

# Scripture Index

www.ingramcontent.com/pod-product-compliance
Lightning Source LLC
Chambersburg PA
CBHW060425090426
42734CB00011B/2445